THE ROAD TO
Emmaus

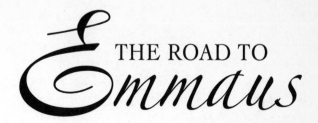

THE ROAD TO

Emmaus

Helen Julian CSF

COMPANIONS FOR THE JOURNEY THROUGH LENT

Published by
The Bible Reading Fellowship
First Floor, Elsfield Hall
15–17 Elsfield Way, Oxford OX2 8FG
Website: www.brf.org.uk

ISBN-10: 1 84101 442 7
ISBN-13: 978 1 84101 442 5
First published 2006
10 9 8 7 6 5 4 3 2 1 0

Acknowledgments
Scripture quotations are taken from The New Revised Standard Version of
the Bible, Anglicized Edition, copyright © 1989, 1995 by the Division of
Christian Education of the National Council of the Churches of Christ in
the USA, and are used by permission. All rights reserved.

A catalogue record for this book is available from the British Library

Printed in Singapore by Craft Print International Ltd

CONTENTS

Lent 3: The Cloud of Unknowing

Lent 4: John and Charles Wesley

Lent 5: John Donne

Holy Week: Julian of Norwich

INTRODUCTION

For many Christians, Lent is a time of heightened and more purposeful engagement with the many elements of the Christian life. It has, of course, a particular focus on discipline, penitence, fasting and reflection on the passion of Christ, but for many it is also a time to overhaul their prayer life, to read the scriptures in a more organized way, and to serve others more consciously.

The seven figures from British spirituality whom you will meet in this book are, I hope, good guides on this pilgrimage through Lent. Through their lives and work, Lenten themes and others can be illuminated. They are all authors, so if any become particular friends and guides to you during this Lenten journey, you can continue to travel with them after finishing this book, by exploring further their own writings.

The journey of this book takes you from joy, the joy of creation, through places of darkness and struggle, and places of light, encouragement and growth, to the rediscovered joy of re-creation.

Along the way there are opportunities to put into practice some of what the companions are offering as their particular gift. Julian of Norwich, with whom we will walk through Holy Week, wrote of her own book, 'This book is begun by God's gift and his grace; but it is not yet performed'.[1] To be really effective, this book needs to be 'performed'; put into practice in ways which engage body, spirit, and mind—which is why you will find a section headed 'Performance' at the end of each week's readings.

All of the suggested activities can be carried out on your own if that is how you are using the book. If you are using it in a group, I recommend that each of you commit yourself to trying at least one of the suggestions each week, and then, when you meet, sharing with each other what you did and how it worked for you. You might also like to share what you found helpful or puzzling in the week's readings. There are no right or wrong answers; anything that draws you closer to God and helps you to reflect on your pilgrimage of faith is valuable.

Don't feel that you have to follow the daily reading format exactly if that doesn't suit you. You may choose to read several days at once, and then have a day or more free to spend on one of the activities.

Our Christian journey is never made alone, however it may sometimes feel. The great company of our fellow travellers extends through time and space; may this Lent be a time when some of these companions become real friends and guides to you.

Thomas Traherne

Ash Wednesday

ENJOYING THE WORLD

In the beginning when God created the heavens and the earth, the earth was a formless void and darkness covered the face of the deep, while a wind from God swept over the face of the waters. Then God said, 'Let there be light'; and there was light. And God saw that the light was good; and God separated the light from the darkness. God called the light Day, and the darkness he called Night. And there was evening and there was morning, the first day…

In the day that the Lord God made the earth and the heavens, when no plant of the field was yet in the earth and no herb of the field had yet sprung up—for the Lord God had not caused it to rain upon the earth, and there was no one to till the ground; but a stream would rise from the earth, and water the whole face of the ground—then the Lord God formed man from the dust of the ground, and breathed into his nostrils the breath of life; and the man became a living being. And the Lord God planted a garden in Eden, in the east; and there he put the man whom he had formed.
GENESIS 1:1–5; 2:4B–8

Today, in churches all over the world, worshippers will have a cross of ash marked on their foreheads. With it go the words, 'Remember you are dust, and to dust you will return', words drawing on this passage of Genesis and used also in the Anglican burial service.

It seems a suitably penitential but perhaps rather depressing start to Lent. It is a reminder of mortality, of the fragility of life, and of the reality that we will all end as anonymous dust, some sooner, some later.

But it can also be a positive reminder that we are created beings, who can celebrate our creation and our Creator. Our very existence rests on the God who formed us and breathed life into us, and who continues to provide us with what we need to live—air and water and light. As Christians, we belong to a faith that values the things of the earth, seeing them as gifts of God. In Lent, in many churches, they are used powerfully for their symbolism: the ash of Ash Wednesday, the oil blessed by the bishop for use in anointing during the coming year, the water for the foot-washing on Maundy Thursday, and the new fire kindled on Easter Day. We are made of the earth, and our life is rooted in it.

Thomas Traherne, our first companion, would have sympathized with this view. He himself died in his 40s, in 1674, and it seemed for a long time that he had joined the company of the anonymous dead. He wrote many meditations, in prose and poetry, but none were published during his lifetime and it was only the chance discovery of a manuscript on a second-hand book barrow in Farringdon Road, London, in 1896 that brought him to a new and appreciative audience.

The known facts of his life are few. He was born in Hereford, around 1637, the son of a shoemaker. He was educated at Brasenose College, Oxford, during the Commonwealth, and then appointed rector of the parish of Credenhill near Hereford, in 1657. When the monarchy was restored, he was ordained in the Anglican Church. In 1667 he became chaplain to the Lord Keeper of the Seals, who had his household at Teddington, Middlesex, and it was there that Traherne died.

With the restoration of the monarchy came also the newly restored Book of Common Prayer, and Traherne valued its emphasis on a regular pattern of prayer with others, made up largely of psalms and scripture. He also valued its sanctification of time through the various seasons, special festivals and saints' days of the year. But it is for his love of creation, above all, that Traherne is known and appreciated today. He always found the world beautiful, writing in his poem 'Nature', 'The world's fair beauty set my soul on fire.'[1] People were not left out of this appreciation: Traherne was gregarious and sociable. In one of his private notebooks he wrote, 'Thou, Lord, hast made thy servant a sociable creature for the praise of thy name; a lover of company.'[2] He always remembered having seen, as a child, an empty banqueting hall transformed as it filled up with 'lords and ladies and music and dancing'. 'I perceived,' he wrote, 'that men and women are, when well understood, a principal part of our true felicity.'[3]

So Traherne enjoyed the world not for himself alone, but also in order to lead others to the same enjoyment. In one of his most famous passages, he writes powerfully of a rapturous enjoyment of the world, an enjoyment made deeper because there are others with whom to share it.

You never enjoy the world aright, till the sea itself floweth in your veins, till you are clothed with the heavens, and crowned with the stars: and perceive yourself to be the sole heir of the whole world, and more than so, because men are in it who are every one sole heirs as well as you. Till you can sing and rejoice and delight in God, as misers do in gold, and kings in sceptres, you never enjoy the world.

Yet further, you never enjoy the world aright, till you so love the beauty of enjoying it, that you are covetous and earnest to persuade others to enjoy it.[4]

PRAYER

Creator God, thank you for having created me, and for sustaining me through your gifts. Make me more aware of your presence in your creation, and eager to bring others to know you. Amen.

Thursday

THE RIGHT TREASURE

Jesus said to his disciples, 'Therefore I tell you, do not worry about your life, what you will eat, or about your body, what you will wear. For life is more than food, and the body more than clothing... Consider the lilies, how they grow: they neither toil nor spin; yet I tell you, even Solomon in all his glory was not clothed like one of these. But if God so clothes the grass of the field, which is alive today and tomorrow is thrown into the oven, how much more will he clothe you—you of little faith! And do not keep striving for what you are to eat and what you are to drink, and do not keep worrying. For it is the nations of the world that strive after all these things, and your Father knows that you need them. Instead, strive for his kingdom, and these things will be given to you as well.

'Do not be afraid, little flock, for it is your Father's good pleasure to give you the kingdom. Sell your possessions, and give alms. Make purses for yourselves that do not wear out, an unfailing treasure in heaven, where no thief comes near and no moth destroys. For where your treasure is, there your heart will be also.'

LUKE 12:22–23, 27–34

There are two ways to be rich: to acquire more possessions and money, or to want less. We can spend our lives and our energy always wanting and working for more, never satisfied with what we have. Much of consumer culture urges this way on us. We are told, subtly or unsubtly, that others will judge us by what we own, and that we must therefore own the latest, the newest, the best of everything. Last year's mobile phone will not do; we must have the one that everyone is talking about—and this despite the fact that many of us never get the hang of most of our gadgets' abilities. Certainly, as I write this, I'm aware of my very basic level of competence with computers, and the tiny part of their capability that I actually use or indeed need.

Our judgment of ourselves can come to rest on this too, making us perpetually dissatisfied and restless, sure that if only we had this or that gadget, could afford to holiday in this year's most fashionable place, or trade our house for one in a better neighbourhood, we would be happy. Even our most personal and intimate decisions can be affected: many couples wait years to be married because they must save up to have the perfect wedding.

The way of the gospel is radically different. Jesus assures us that we will not go hungry or naked; God knows that we need these things and will provide them. But we are not to make clothes, food, or anything else created into our 'treasure'. Released from the worry of depending entirely on ourselves and our efforts, we can put our energy and our hearts into the service of God and into work for his kingdom.

Thomas Traherne followed the gospel way of thinking. He saw God and God's goodness in every part of creation—in the immensity of the sun, the stars and all the heavens, but also in a drop of water, an apple, a grain of sand or an ear of corn. All was gift; 'it proceedeth from the most perfect Lover to the most perfectly Beloved'.[5]

'It is your Father's good pleasure to give you the kingdom,' said Jesus, and Traherne expanded on these words.

To know God is life eternal. To know God is to know goodness; it is to see the beauty of infinite love; to see it attended with almighty power and eternal wisdom. It is to see the king of heaven and earth take infinite delight in giving. He is not an object of terror, but delight. To know him therefore as he is, is to frame the most beautiful idea in all worlds. He delights in our happiness more than we do. An infinite Lord, who, having all riches, honours and pleasures in his own hand, is infinitely willing to give them unto me.[6]

The upside-down world of the gospel, where the poor and the hungry are blessed, was one in which Traherne felt at home. What God supplied in abundance was the truly valuable: 'it must be in accordance with his nature that the best things should be the most common and only things which are worthless scarce'.[7] In a world of market forces, where the laws of supply and demand rule, and where scarce things are valued simply because most people cannot have them, this is a radical view.

Traherne felt that he was rich in his 'possession' of the things that all could share. It seems that he lived by these beliefs, spending the last ten years of his life as a member of someone else's household, without a home of his own. When he died, he left a few bequests of money, and his books and his best hat to his brother. He had been rich in his appreciation of God, 'the most perfect Lover' and the giver of all that was needed for life.

PRAYER

Generous God, let me know you as Lover and myself as Beloved today. Open my eyes to see the gifts that you shower upon me, and the real riches that are already mine. Amen.

Friday

THE THRONE OF LOVE

[Jesus continued] 'Now my soul is troubled. And what should I say—"Father, save me from this hour"? No, it is for this reason that I have come to this hour. Father, glorify your name.' Then a voice came from heaven, 'I have glorified it, and I will glorify it again.' The crowd standing there heard it and said that it was thunder. Others said, 'An angel has spoken to him.' Jesus answered, 'This voice has come for your sake, not for mine. Now is the judgment of this world; now the ruler of this world will be driven out. And I, when I am lifted up from the earth, will draw all people to myself.' He said this to indicate the kind of death he was to die. The crowd answered him, 'We have heard from the law that the Messiah remains for ever. How can you say that the Son of Man must be lifted up. Who is this Son of Man?' Jesus said to them, 'The light is with you for a little longer. Walk while you have the light, so that the darkness may not overtake you. If you walk in the darkness, you do not know where you are going. While you have the light, believe in the light, so that you may become children of light.'

JOHN 12:27–36

In John's Gospel, cross and glory are inextricably linked. The crucifixion is not a disaster, which is then followed by the resurrection, making it into a triumph. In 'this hour' God's name is glorified, and all people are drawn to the place of their redemption. Light and darkness are both present, but as John says in his Prologue, 'The light shines in the darkness, and the darkness did not overcome it' (John 1:5).

In the early centuries of Christianity, it was common to depict Christ on the cross not as the agonized victim of a cruel form of punishment and death, but as a king, crowned and robed, reigning from the tree. You can find this image in some of the very early hymns too. For example, in 'The royal banners forward go', written in the sixth century, we find the verse:

Fulfilled is all that David told
In true prophetic song of old;
Amidst the nations, God, saith he,
Has reigned and triumphed from the tree.[8]

Traherne is in this tradition. Although his main emphasis is on the joy and beauty of creation, he does not deny the reality of sin, and so there is need of a remedy for sin. But he rarely lingers at the cross, and when he does, he sees it very clearly as a place of glory as well as of suffering.

In his poem 'An hymn upon St Bartholomew's Day' he exhorts, 'O fly my Soul and haste away to Jesus' Throne or Cross',[9] and in one of his meditations he writes, 'The cross is the abyss of wonders, the centre of desires, the school of virtues, the house of wisdom, the throne of love, the theatre of joys and the place of sorrows. It is the root of happiness and the gate of heaven.'[10] In other places he describes it as 'the most exalted of all objects', 'the Jacob's ladder by which we ascend into the highest heaven', and 'a tree set on fire with invisible flame… The flame is love'.[11]

That love is the love that led Christ to the cross. As Traherne sees God's love behind all the gifts of creation, so he sees the passion as the ultimate expression of divine love.

These two properties are in love, that it can attempt all and suffer all. And the more it suffers the more it is delighted, and the more it attempteth the more it is enriched, for it seems that all love is so mysterious, that there is something in it which needs expression, and can never be understood by any manifestation of itself, in itself, but only by mighty doings and sufferings... This moved God the Father to create the world, and God the Son to die for it.[12]

Yet just as the enjoyment of creation is not complete until we rejoice that others share it, so our redemption by the cross is not for ourselves alone. In his poem 'Mankind is sick', Traherne writes movingly about how those who are made whole must be willing to act as physicians to those still diseased. God's love is infinite, and by sharing it with others we can still have all we desire for ourselves.

What would we give! that they might likewise see
    The glory of his majesty!
The joy and fullness of that high delight,
    Whose blessedness is infinite!
    We would even cease to live, to gain
    Them from their misery and pain,
        And make them with us reign.
For they themselves would be our greatest treasures
    When sav'd, our own most heavenly pleasures.[13]

Those of us who know the light and who, by God's grace, walk in the light, have a responsibility to those still in darkness, and this can be a source of joy for us.

PRAYER

God of compassion, thank you for all that you do in your love, and especially for your passion, death and resurrection. Give me a share in your passion for the world, that I may bring others into your kingdom, leading them to become children of light. Amen.

Saturday

AS A CHILD

People were bringing little children to Jesus in order that he might touch them; and the disciples spoke sternly to them. But when Jesus saw this, he was indignant and said to them, 'Let the little children come to me; do not stop them; for it is to such as these that the kingdom of God belongs. Truly I tell you, whoever does not receive the kingdom of God as a little child will never enter it.' And he took them up in his arms, laid his hands on them, and blessed them.

MARK 10:13–16

A while ago I visited a friend who had a daughter approaching her first birthday. We went together to the beach and my friend and I sat talking. After a while I noticed that the child, sitting beside us, was picking up each pebble within reach in turn, and inspecting it closely. Then she would put it down and pick up the next. What to me was just a pebbly beach, on which it was rather difficult to sit comfortably, was to her a source of endless fascination.

Thomas Traherne, unusually, kept to the end of his life that vivid perception of reality which seems to come naturally to children, but which most of us lose as we grow up.

The pure and unsullied perception I had from the womb and that divine light with which I was born are to this day the best in which I can see the universe. By the gift of God they attended me into the world and by his especial favour I remember them still. Everything appeared new and

21

strange at first, inexpressibly rare, delightful and beautiful. I was a little stranger who at my entrance into the world was saluted and surrounded by innumerable joys.[14]

Like most of us, at first he lost this natural gift of wonder, buried under the weight of an education that 'did not foster and cherish it',[15] and swamped by a world that did not seem to see things this way or to value time spent simply looking and appreciating. The light was eclipsed, however, not destroyed totally, and so he was able to find it again, and many of his poems are written from this perspective. The poem 'Wonder' begins:

How like an Angel came I down!
How bright are all things here!
When first among his works I did appear
O how their glory me did crown![16]

Far from casting off childish ways as he grew up, he saw childhood as 'my tutor, teacher, guide'.[17] He often uses the metaphor of sight to describe the child's approach to the world, of clear sight and opened eyes, although, as this extract from 'The Preparative' makes clear, he was very aware of all the senses.

For sight inherits beauty; hearing, sounds;
    The nostril, sweet perfumes,
    All tastes have hidden rooms
Within the tongue; the feeling feeling wounds
    With pleasure and delight: but I
Forgot the rest, and was all sight or eye...[18]

At the end of the same poem, he declares, 'Felicity appears to none but them that purely see.' Seeing clearly is, for Traherne, a foretaste of heaven. He boldly declares, 'We need nothing but open eyes to be ravished like the Cherubims'.[19]

Those open eyes are still possible. It's easy to dismiss Traherne's vision as coming from a simpler, pre-industrial age, when most people lived much more closely with the natural world. But there are those today who can still recapture his direct engagement with the natural world.

Writing in the 20th century about why childhood memories of nature can be particularly strong, Edward Thomas describes the child's view of a tree:

... [not] a column of dark stony substance supporting a number of green wagers that live scarcely half a year, and grown for the manufacture of furniture, gates, and many other things; but we saw something quite unlike ourselves, large, gentle, of foreign tongue, without locomotion, yet full of life and movement and sound of the leaves themselves, and also of the light, of the birds, and of the insects; and they were givers of clear, deep joy that cannot be expressed.[20]

Perhaps it is this clear, direct seeing that makes us able to enter the kingdom, to see God at work within the very ordinary experiences of our days. Then we realize that the kingdom is already at work within and around us, and that in seeing aright, we are already part of it.

PRAYER

Gracious God, give me the sight of a child again, that I may see you in your creation and, with open eyes, see your kingdom already coming in our world. Amen.

A WALK OF AWARENESS

Begin by offering the time of the walk to God to use. Give thanks for the place where you will be walking, and for the opportunity to spend time with God's creation; and open yourself to the working of the Spirit.

Then, as Thomas Traherne puts it, 'By an act of understanding therefore be present now with all the creatures among which you live, and hear them in their beings and operations praising God in an heavenly manner; some of them vocally, others in their ministry, all of them naturally and continually.'[21]

As you step outside, take a moment to be conscious of the air and of your breathing. Every breath is God's gift of life. Give thanks for the weather—whatever it's like. Pray with Traherne: 'Let all thy creatures bless thee, O Lord, and my soul praise and bless thee for them all.'[22]

Take a moment to be conscious of the earth beneath your feet.

Walk slowly and mindfully; this is not walking to reach a destination, or to exercise off your lunch. Give yourself plenty of time to notice everything that is around you.

When something particularly catches your eye, stop walking and give it your full attention. Try to see it afresh, as if for the first time, like a child:

A child's world is fresh and new and beautiful, full of wonder and excitement. It is our misfortune that for most of us that clear-eyed vision, that true instinct for what is beautiful and awe-inspiring, is dimmed and even lost before we reach adulthood.

RACHEL CARSON, *THE SENSE OF WONDER* (HARPER & ROW, 1956), P. 42

Pay attention to the small, commonplace and simple as well as to the grand or the unusual—to the sparrow as well as the kingfisher; to the blade of grass as well as the tree; to the daisy as well as the orchid.

Use all your senses—touch, taste, hear, smell and see.

> I that so long
> Was nothing from eternity,
> Did little think such joys as ear and tongue
> To celebrate or see:
> Such sounds to hear, such hands to feel, such feet,
> Beneath the skies, on such a ground to meet.[23]

What can you see of the goodness of God in this particular part of God's creation? Delight in it, and give thanks to God for it.

Then move further on your walk, again giving your attention to what is around you, until something else captures your attention. End your walk in praise to God the Creator:

I give thee thanks for the beauty of colours, for the harmony of sounds, for the pleasantness of odours, for the sweetness of food, for the warmth and softness of our raiment, and for all my five senses, and all the pores of my body, so curiously made, and for the preservation as well as use of all my limbs and senses.[24]

THROUGH THE EYES OF A CHILD

Set aside some time this week to spend with a small child. If you don't have one of your own, borrow one from family or friends! You'll be giving their carers the gift of some time free from parental responsibility, as well as giving yourself the gift of time with someone who still sees with open eyes.

Choose a simple activity—go to the duck pond, walk in the woods, play in the garden, enjoy bath time—and consciously set yourself to see the world through the eyes of the child. Slow down;

take an interest in what he or she is interested in; laugh together.

At the end of the day, reflect on what you've learnt. Can you think of ways to build this kind of seeing into your daily routine?

SPENDING AND GETTING

Whenever you shop this week, take a little time beforehand to consider why you are buying what you are buying. Have you been influenced by advertisements, special promotions, or pressure from children or from your peer group, into buying something you don't really want or need? Particularly if you are replacing something you already have, ask yourself whether the existing machine or gadget has really reached the end of its life, and whether you really need the extra capacity of whatever you are planning to buy.

Take some time during the week to thank God for all that he gives you. Start with the universal gifts that we often take for granted: air, water, light. Then move on to the gifts he has given specifically to you: people who care for you and those for whom you care, talents you can use to enrich your own life and the lives of others, freedom to worship with others. Make a conscious act of trust in God's care for you, hearing Jesus' words, 'Strive for his kingdom, and these things will be given to you as well.'

The Venerable Bede

Sunday

ALL THINGS IN COMMON

Awe came upon everyone, because many wonders and signs were being done by the apostles. All who believed were together and had all things in common; they would sell their possessions and goods and distribute the proceeds to all, as any had need. Day by day, as they spent much time together in the temple, they broke bread at home and ate their food with glad and generous hearts, praising God and having the goodwill of all the people. And day by day the Lord added to their number those who were being saved.

ACTS 2:43–47

This is a text that our second companion, Bede, would have heard often. The story of the early church's way of life was one of the foundation texts for the monastic life that he followed for around 55 years—almost the whole of his life.

Bede was born in the north of England around AD673, and at the age of seven was sent to the recently founded monastery at Monkwearmouth, at the mouth of the River Tyne. He spent the rest of his life there, as part of a twin monastery. The second community was founded just after Bede arrived, at Jarrow, about seven miles north.

It would seem very odd to us today for a child of seven to be sent to a monastery, but at that time monasteries were the main source of education. Bede would have learnt to read and write in Latin, using the books of the Bible to do so, and seems to have taken well to learning: in a brief autobiography attached to his most famous book, *The Ecclesiastical History of the English People*, he says, 'My chief delight has always been in study, teaching and writing'.[1] It is this autobiography that tells us nearly everything we know about Bede. He gives pride of place to a list of the books that he wrote—around 30 of them. They were popular and in great demand in his own day and afterwards and, in contrast to Traherne's obscurity, Bede has never fallen out of favour. Of the books he lists, only one has not survived; and most survive in a number of manuscripts.

Bede was one of the first people to write on the Acts of the Apostles, and in fact did so twice. He would have spent time pondering this passage, and certainly he held the example of the early church in high esteem as a model for how the church of his own day should live.

Bede describes how Augustine and his companions, sent from Rome to bring the gospel to Britain, arrived in Canterbury in 597 and were given a house by the king: 'As soon as they had occupied the house given to them they began to emulate the life of the apostles and the primitive church. They were constantly at prayer; they fasted and kept vigils; they preached the word of life to whomsoever they could.'[2] And he records the answer given by Pope Gregory, who had sent Augustine to Britain, to a question about how the clergy should live. 'You are therefore,' Gregory wrote, 'to follow the way of life practised by our forefathers of the primitive Church, who regarded no property as personal, but shared all things in common.'[3]

The religious life was not just for men. Bede also tells the story of Hilda, one of the first British women to take religious vows. She was a member of the royal family, and became a nun at the age of 33. Obviously a very able woman, she became abbess first of Hartlepool and then of Whitby, which she founded. Bede says, 'After the example of the primitive Church, no one there was rich or poor, for everything was held in common, and none possessed any personal property.'[4]

The common life which was at the heart of the many monasteries of Anglo-Saxon England was intended to build up a community that could demonstrate Christ's love, first within the monastery itself and then to those outside. As with the early apostles in the book of Acts, there was a strong missionary impulse among the monks and nuns of Bede's time. They wanted to live the gospel in all its fullness, in order to bring others into the fullness of life that Jesus promised. In a homily for the dedication of a church, Bede puts it beautifully.

We must not suppose that only the building in which we come together to pray and celebrate the mysteries is the Lord's temple, for we ourselves who come together in the Lord's name are more fully his temple... Let us busy ourselves in building an eternal mansion by the mutual help of charity so that when our Lord Jesus Christ comes he may find us all with cheerful hearts and tireless in doing all the good which he has commanded us to do.[5]

PRAYER

God of grace, you called Bede into community to work and to worship, to learn and to teach. Draw me more closely into your body, that in mutual love and fellowship I may do your work and follow your will. Amen.

Monday

FAITHFUL TO THE FAITHFUL GOD

But we appeal to you, brothers and sisters, to respect those who labour among you, and have charge of you in the Lord and admonish you; esteem them very highly in love because of their work. Be at peace among yourselves. And we urge you, beloved, to admonish the idlers, encourage the faint-hearted, help the weak, be patient with all of them. See that none of you repays evil for evil, but always seek to do good to one another and to all. Rejoice always, pray without ceasing, give thanks in all circumstances; for this is the will of God in Christ Jesus for you... The one who calls you is faithful, and he will do this.

1 THESSALONIANS 5:12–18, 24

Although all that we know for certain about Bede comes in the few pages at the end of the *Ecclesiastical History*, there may be occasional glimpses in other writings. For example, there is a story in the anonymous *History of Abbot Ceolfrith*, first abbot of the monastery of Jarrow, which is usually believed to refer to Bede. In 686, plague struck the monastery:

All those who could read or preach or were able to sing the antiphons and responsories were carried off by the plague except the abbot himself and one small boy, who had been brought up and taught by him and who until the present day holds the rank of a priest in the same monastery... Because of the plague the abbot was very sorrowful and ordered the previous custom to be interrupted and that the whole psalter except at

Lauds and Vespers should be recited without antiphons. But when this was done for the space of only one week with many tears and laments, he felt unable to bear it any longer so he decided that the psalms with antiphons should be resumed as before. With everyone trying their best, he completed this by himself but with the help of the boy mentioned above, with no small labour. [6]

Prayer was at the very heart of the work of the monastery, and not even the plague could prevent it from being offered with care and devotion. If the small boy was indeed Bede, he must have been naturally scholarly to have been able to assist the abbot in this way. There is some evidence that this was the case in the fact that he was made deacon at the age of 19, six years before the usual age. He became a priest when he was 30. All this took place in the monastery at Jarrow, to which he had been transferred from Monkwearmouth.

Not all monks spent all their life in one monastery. In his *Lives of the Abbots*, Bede recounts the travels of some of the abbots of his monastery. Benedict Biscop, for example, first abbot of Monkwear-mouth, made a number of visits to Rome. After one of them, he spent two years at a monastery in France before returning to Rome and then accompanying Theodore, newly consecrated archbishop, back to Canterbury, where he became abbot of St Peter's monastery for two years. He then visited Rome again, and on his return founded the monastery of Monkwearmouth. Soon he was off to France to find stonemasons for the new monastery church, and made two further journeys to Rome, returning each time with books, relics, pictures and other items to enrich the life and worship of his monks.

Bede, in contrast, made very few journeys outside his own monastery. He certainly went to Lindisfarne at least once when he was writing his *Life of St Cuthbert* and we know of a visit to York and one to the monastery of Abbot Wihtred.

The daily life of the monastery, with its regular times of worship and its hours set aside for study and for work (in Bede's case, largely writing and teaching) seems to have satisfied him. Even in his old age he wanted to take part fully in the life, and to remain faithful to the vows he had made as a young man. Alcuin, a deacon, scholar and teacher from York, recorded this story:

When Bede was asked why he was so diligent in attending Office in old age he said: I know that the angels visit the canonical hours in the congregation of the brethren. What if they do not find me among them? Will they not say, where is Bede? Why does he not come to the prescribed devotions of the brothers?' [7]

The presence of every person mattered, and so faithfulness mattered. God's faithfulness was to be repaid with human faithfulness. Bede was faithful to God and to prayer until the end of his life. A letter written about his death records that he asked the monk with him:

'Hold my head in your hands for it is a great delight for me to sit over against my holy place in which I used to pray, that as I sit there I may call upon my Father.' And so, upon the floor of his cell, singing, 'Glory be to the Father and to the Son and to the Holy Spirit' and the rest, he breathed his last. [8]

PRAYER

Make these words of Bede the subject of your prayer and meditation, as you reflect on God's faithfulness, and your response.

'Christ is the morning star who, when the night of this world is past, promises and reveals to his saints the light of life and of everlasting day.'

Tuesday

GOD OF HISTORY

O give thanks to the Lord, call upon his name, make known his deeds among the peoples. Sing to him, sing praises to him; tell of all his wonderful works... Remember the wonderful works he has done, his miracles, and the judgments he uttered, O offspring of his servant Abraham, children of Jacob, his chosen ones... When they were few in number, of little account, and strangers in it, wandering from nation to nation, from one kingdom to another people, he allowed no one to oppress them; he rebuked kings on their account... Then he brought Israel out with silver and gold, and there was no one among their tribes who stumbled... So he brought his people out with joy, his chosen ones with singing. He gave them the lands of the nations, and they took possession of the wealth of the peoples, that they might keep his statutes and observe his laws. Praise the Lord!

PSALM 105:1–2, 5–6, 12–14, 37, 43–45

Bede's *Ecclesiastical History* was his most copied book: there are more than 130 complete manuscripts still in existence. Written in Latin, as were all his books, it was translated into English at the time of King Alfred. When printing became available, it was still in demand, and had been printed three times by 1507. It covers the story of England from the end of the Roman occupation until the year of its writing, 731.

Bede's view of history is very much in tune with that of the Bible. Biblical history is always told with a purpose, and that purpose is theological, and so it was with Bede. For the biblical writers, history is the place of God's activity, and it is God who acts to save his people, to free them from bondage to slavery and to bring them into the promised land.

One writer on Bede suggests that we should see the *Ecclesiastical History* not as a different kind of work from most of Bede's previous books, which were biblical commentaries, but as the climax to them, and the last of the commentaries. Bede chose the books on which he wrote his commentaries carefully to serve a purpose: to help in the work of establishing the church, and especially its priesthood, on earth. 'The Song of Songs, for instance, was regarded as an allegory of the relations between Christ and the Church; Samuel was the great judge and priest of Israel who anointed kings; Solomon's Temple and Tabernacle were obvious allegories for the building up of the Church.' [9]

But it was the Acts of the Apostles that gave Bede the great theme of his *History*. As it shaped the life of the monastery, so it gave him a shape for the work that was in some way a summary of all his work. Luke, in the book of Acts, had chronicled the gradual triumph of the Christian faith among the people of his world, and the forming of a new people of God whose destiny was to preach the gospel to the ends of the earth. Bede chronicles the growth of Christianity among the pagan peoples of Britain, and their missionary fervour to take the gospel beyond their own shores.

Certainly his *History* had a moral purpose. In his preface he writes:

For if history records good things of good men, the thoughtful hearer is encouraged to imitate what is good: or if it records evil of wicked men, the good religious listener or reader is encouraged to avoid all that is sinful and perverse, and to follow what he knows to be good and pleasing to God. [10]

The Bible is the background to all of Bede's writing, and he naturally draws examples and comparisons from it. For Bede, the people of

Britain are God's new people, no less than the people of Israel are shown as God's people in the Bible. The process of building a Christian country was a slow one, with many setbacks, recalling the rocky story of God's covenant with his chosen people in the Old Testament. As the kings in the historical books of the Old Testament are judged by their faithfulness and obedience to God rather than their worldly success or lack of it, so are the kings in Bede's history. Often it was the king's conversion that led to the conversion of his whole kingdom, but if he then fell away, the faith of a whole people was at risk. Bad kings usually come to a bad end in Bede's *History*, but even this does not always bring the people back to the faith.

Bede has been called the 'father of English history' but it is a very particular kind of history. Like the Bible which was his inspiration, it is a history of salvation, a history in which God takes centre stage, and in which the heroes are often simple bishops and monks rather than warrior kings.

PRAYER

God of history, thank you for all that you have done through the centuries to draw peoples and nations to yourself, and to keep them in the faith. Open my eyes to see you at work in today's world, and to see what part I have to play in bringing in your kingdom on earth. Amen.

Wednesday

GOD AT WORK

Listen to me, you that pursue righteousness, you that seek the
Lord. Look to the rock from which you were hewn, and to the
quarry from which you were dug. Look to Abraham your father
and to Sarah who bore you; for he was but one when I called him,
but I blessed him and made him many.

ISAIAH 51:1–2

We have begun to look at Bede's historical writing; and recognized
that it had a moral purpose. Now it is time to delve a little deeper.
What beliefs informed his writing? What determined his decisions
about what to include and what to leave out? And how did a single
monk, who rarely left his monastery in the north of England, come
to know so much about several hundred years of his country's
history?

Bede himself wanted to assure his readers that he had good
sources for what he wrote. In his preface, he carefully lists the
people who have helped him. In particular he thanks Abbot Albinus
of Canterbury, and Nothelm, a priest in London, for information
about the church in Canterbury. In addition, Nothelm visited the
papal archives in Rome, and brought back copies of relevant letters.
Bishop Daniel of the West Saxons sent information about the
church in his own province, and the brothers of Lastingham
monastery supplied the stories of their founders, Cedd and Ceadda.
Bishop Cynebert supplied the story of the church in the province
of Lindsey.

When it came to Bede's own territory of Northumbria, he was able to draw on 'countless faithful witnesses who either know or remember the facts'.[11] We can see from his list how central the church was in his view of the history of his country.

Some of what these witnesses sent Bede would be strictly factual —which kings reigned when, what battles they took part in and the outcome, the founding of dioceses and of monasteries, the conversion or apostasy of kings and people. But they would also have sent details of local saints and their miracles, and this is where the theological nature of Bede's history becomes very clear. The world he is writing about is God's world, and God can intervene when he chooses, to bring about miraculous healings or to give one of his saints prophetic knowledge. Again, Bede is concerned that his readers should know his sources, and so he will state whether he is simply recording a traditional story or whether he has heard the story from an eyewitness, or someone who had met either the saint or the beneficiary of the miracle. He does the same in his biography (or, more properly, hagiography) of Saint Cuthbert. Because Cuthbert was a Northumbrian who had died around the time Bede was born, Bede often had direct contact with those who had known the saint, and so could say, 'I was told this story by so-and-so, who is now a priest in this monastery.'

In both history and hagiography, it is initially disconcerting to find miracle stories that are obvious copies of Gospel stories, and others that are copied directly from the lives of earlier saints. The writer here is concerned with a deeper question than simply 'Did this actually happen exactly as I am telling it?' The point of miracle stories is to make it clear that the one working the miracles was a holy man or woman who had God's favour, and who could therefore draw on God's power. The reader needs to approach them with the same frame of mind as the reader of the Bible, asking not so much, 'Did this happen in exactly this way?' but 'Why is the author telling me this at this point?'

Another underlying (and commonly held) belief that shaped Bede's historical writing was that the end of the world would come soon. He quotes a letter sent by Pope Gregory I to King Ethelbert: 'We would also have Your Majesty know what we have learned from the words of Almighty God in holy Scripture, that the end of this present world and the eternal kingdom of the Saints is approaching.'[12]

Some thought that the end would come in AD1000, others that the date could not be calculated. This belief about the end of the world came from the doctrine of the six ages of world history, each starting with a major biblical event or person: the creation, the flood, Abraham, David, the Babylonian captivity, and the incarnation of Christ. Christians therefore were living in the last age, a belief familiar to many of the New Testament writers, and this gave a sense of urgency to all their work. In his commentaries, Bede often speaks of those who are 'snatched' from the devil, and in his own life he expressed this urgency, teaching his pupils up to the day before he died, and saying to them, 'Learn speedily, I know not how long I shall be with you.'[13]

Bede's historical writings were set in the context of faith and against the background of God's dealings with his people from the beginning until the present. Although Bede would not have said so, in a way his history was a further 'testament', a witness to God's work in his world.

PRAYER

God of time and of eternity, help me to see all human history in the context of your love and of your desire that everyone should come to know you. Give me a sense of urgency to do your work. Amen.

Thursday

THE BREAD OF THE WORD

Therefore take up the whole armour of God, so that you may be able to withstand on that evil day, and having done everything, to stand firm. Stand therefore, and fasten the belt of truth around your waist, and put on the breastplate of righteousness. As shoes for your feet put on whatever will make you ready to proclaim the gospel of peace. With all of these, take the shield of faith, with which you will be able to quench all the flaming arrows of the evil one. Take the helmet of salvation, and the sword of the Spirit, which is the word of God.

EPHESIANS 6:13–17

In Bede's time, monasteries were not only centres of prayer but also of learning. There were no universities or publishing houses, and very few libraries. It was the clergy—in particular, monks—who had the education and the time to study and to write, and it was very often in the monasteries that books were copied. There was no printing, of course, so books had to be copied by hand, and this was a time-consuming process. With no artificial light, the work could only be done in daylight and, especially in the north, it was sometimes too cold for the scribes to work.

The Lindisfarne Gospels, a particularly beautifully decorated book made in honour of St Cuthbert around the end of the seventh century, probably took at least five years to make. But even much smaller and simpler books represent many hours of skilled work. Hence, books were rare and expensive, and the libraries in monasteries were very small by our standards. Bede, who was the most widely read man of his day, is known to have used 175 titles, and the library at Jarrow may perhaps have held three times that number of volumes.

The Bible was, of course, the most important book in any monastic library, and copies of the scriptures and commentaries on them would have made up most of the stock. Entire Bibles were rare, and usually separate collection of books were made, such as the epistles or the historical books of the Old Testament. These collec-tions were both more portable and cheaper to make. Latin was the main language used; Bede also consulted a Greek text for some of his commentaries, and was aware of the Hebrew originals, although he did not himself read Hebrew. When most of us can have several copies of the Bible for our personal use if we wish, it's hard to imagine a time when many Christians had no access to the Bible at all, and others to only one copy of the Gospels, kept in the church and shared with many others.

Of course, only a minority of people were literate and, for the many who could not read, the Bible would have been heard in the context of church services and of preaching. Even for those who could read, this use of the Bible in worship provided the framework for their study and writing. Bede wrote his commentaries as 'meditations on the Scriptures leading to conversion of life through prayer'.[14] He read not only the Bible, but commentaries already written by the Fathers of the church such as Augustine and Gregory. He would have known much of the Bible by heart, through constantly hearing and reciting it in church, and often put together sentences from different books to shed new light on each. God was seen as the author of every book in the Bible, and so it was legitimate to use any part to comment on any other.

Bede's usual method was to begin with a careful examination of the text, with reference to the original languages if possible, then to establish what happened or was being said, moving on to look at the particular text in the light of the rest of scripture, and then (especially for Old Testament texts) to consider what the text said about Christ, and how it applied to the reader's own life.

He also studied and wrote on another level, that of the 'spiritual sense', which traditionally had four aspects: the historical (what actually happened), the allegorical (looking for the presence of Christ or the sacraments), the tropological (moral instruction and correction), and the anagogical (looking to the life of heaven and future rewards).[15] This sounds complex and abstract, but Bede wanted everyone to be able to appreciate the scriptures, so he put the idea into a homely simile in his commentary on 1 Samuel.

We are being nourished on food roasted on the gridiron when we understand literally, openly and without any covering, the things in the Scriptures that are said or done for the health of the soul; we eat food from a frying pan when by frequently turning it over we see what allegorically corresponds to the mysteries of Christ; and afterwards we search the oven for bread of the Word to lay hold of the mystical riches of the Scriptures.[16]

PRAYER (WRITTEN BY BEDE)

I pray you, good Jesus, as you have graciously granted me sweet draughts of the Word which tells of you, so you will of your goodness grant that I may come at length to you, the fount of all goodness, and stand before your face for ever.[17]

Friday

A BELIEVING TEACHER

But as for you, continue in what you have learned and firmly believed, knowing from whom you learned it, and how from childhood you have known the sacred writings that are able to instruct you for salvation through faith in Christ Jesus. All scripture is inspired by God and is useful for teaching, for reproof, for correction, and for training in righteousness, so that everyone who belongs to God may be proficient, equipped for every good work. In the presence of God and of Christ Jesus, who is to judge the living and the dead, and in view of his appearing and his kingdom, I solemnly urge you: proclaim the message; be persistent whether the time is favourable or unfavourable; convince, rebuke, and encourage, with the utmost patience in teaching.

2 TIMOTHY 3:14—4:2

Bede's commentaries are very rich in layers of meaning, but they are always informed by his 'sense of urgency, of longing and desire for the presence of Christ in the England of his own times'.[18] The words of Paul to Timothy, '… how from childhood you have known the sacred writings', could have been applied to him very well. He was also eager to 'proclaim the message' as writer and teacher, and as preacher.

Many people could not read Bede's commentaries for themselves, and it was through preaching that the fruit of his work and that of other scholars was shared. As a priest of the monastery, Bede would have preached in the monastery church, to which local people as well as the monks came to worship. He lists two books of homilies on the gospel among his books.

He wrote with admiration of monks who went out of their monasteries to preach the gospel to those far away. St Cuthbert was particularly noted for this activity, and Bede wrote of him:

Cuthbert often went round the villages, sometimes on horseback but more often on foot, preaching the way of truth to those who had gone astray... He made a point of seeking out the steep rugged places in the hills which other preachers dreaded to visit because of their poverty and squalor. He was so eager to preach that he would sometimes be away a whole week or fortnight, or even a month, living among the rough hill folk, preaching and calling them heavenward by his example.[19]

Bede has a lovely image of preachers, which also shows how he interpreted the Bible creatively. In his commentary on Tobit 30:1, 'As they were nearing home, the dog which had been with him on the way ran ahead, as if bringing the news, and wagging his tail', he comments:

This dog, which was a traveller and a companion of an angel, is like a preacher of the gospel, running ahead to announce salvation. Preachers also keep watch over souls committed to them, just as it is natural for dogs to repay those who are kind to them and watch always for the master's safety. And as the dog showed its joy by wagging its tail which is at the end of its body, so every sincerely believing teacher, who is a messenger of the truth, rejoices that his work is accomplished when he leads his people home.[20]

As a 'sincerely believing teacher', he taught the boys who came to the monastery for education, as he himself had done. Latin was the main subject, in order that the trainee monks could learn to say and sing the office, read the Bible, study commentaries on it, preach, and become teachers. Bede also wrote books on grammar, on metre, on figures of speech, on 'The Nature of Things' (that is, natural science) and on time, which included calculation, so we can assume that he also taught these subjects.

Bede saw the availability of teaching on the scriptures as a great source of happiness. Writing about the arrival of Theodore from Rome to become Archbishop of Canterbury in 669, he notes that Theodore and Hadrian, who accompanied him, were men of learning who attracted a large number of students: 'Never had there been such happy times as these since the English settled in Britain... The people eagerly sought the new-found joys of the kingdom of heaven, and all who wished for instruction in the reading of the Scriptures found teachers ready at hand.'[21]

Preaching was not only verbal but also visual. Those who visited Rome brought back pictures, along with books, to adorn the church; 'thus, all who entered the church, even those who could not read, were able, whichever way they looked, to contemplate the dear face of Christ and his saints, even if only in a picture, to put themselves more firmly in mind of the Lord's incarnation'.[22] Every means should be used to make God's word and the knowledge of God's works available to everyone.

PRAYER

Teach me, O God, to value your word above all else, to read it with joy, to meditate upon it with diligence, to share it with others, and to put it into practice in my own life. Amen.

Saturday

CONSTANT PRAISE

I will bless the Lord at all times; his praise shall continually be in my mouth. My soul makes its boast in the Lord; let the humble hear and be glad. O magnify the Lord with me, and let us exalt his name together. I sought the Lord, and he answered me, and delivered me from all my fears. Look to him, and be radiant; so your faces shall never be ashamed. This poor soul cried, and was heard by the Lord, and was saved from every trouble. The angel of the Lord encamps around those who fear him, and delivers them. O taste and see that the Lord is good; happy are those who take refuge in him. O fear the Lord, you his holy ones, for those who fear him have no want. The young lions suffer want and hunger, but those who seek the Lord lack no good thing.

PSALM 34:1–10

Of all the books of the Bible, the Psalms would have been the most familiar to Bede, and probably the first part he would have learnt by heart. They were the kernel of the services prayed by monks, traditionally seven times a day (this practice itself based on a psalm verse: 'Seven times a day I praise you', Psalm 119:164). The whole psalter, 150 psalms, was recited every week, and if the story of the boy who kept up the singing of the offices at Jarrow after the plague is a story of Bede, then by the age of 13 he was obviously competent in both chanting and reading the Psalms.

He would have benefited from the teaching of John, chief singer of the church of St Peter in Rome. John had travelled from Rome with Benedict Biscop and Ceolfrith in 680, the year Bede entered the monastery, with instructions to teach the monks of Monkwearmouth to sing as they did in Rome. Bede records that 'Abbot John taught the cantors of the monastery the theory and practice of singing and reading aloud, and he put into writing all that was necessary for the proper observance of festivals throughout the year. His teachings are still followed in this monastery, and many copies have been made for other places.'[23] It was considered worthwhile bringing someone all the way from Rome, a very long journey and not without dangers, to improve the skills of the monks in this central part of their prayer.

Although they come from the Old Testament, each psalm was seen as a prophecy of Christ, as they were believed to have been composed by David, an ancestor of Jesus. The antiphons, which Ceolfrith was so distressed at being unable to sing after the plague, were composed to emphasize this interpretation of the psalms. The antiphon was used as a kind of refrain, with a trained singer singing the verses of the psalm, and the antiphon sung as a chorus by everyone present either at the beginning and end, or after every group of verses. A collect at the end of each psalm or group of psalms gathered up or collected (hence the name) the sense of each psalm, and directed it in prayer towards Christ.

But the psalms were not used only for public prayer. Alcuin, born in the year that Bede died, writes of the psalms as complete prayer:

In the psalms if you look carefully you will find an intimacy of prayer such as you could never discover by yourself. In the psalms you will find an intimate confession of your sins and a perfect supplication for divine mercy. In the psalms you will find an intimate thanksgiving for all that befalls you. In the psalms you confess your weakness and misery and thereby call down God's mercy upon you. In the psalms you will find every virtue if you are worthy of God's mercy in showing you their secrets.[24]

Many monks used the psalms in their own private prayer, so they became a prayer from the heart. Ceolfrith recited the psalter twice daily in addition to the offices. Bede records that Cuthbert, when abbot of Lindisfarne, would do his rounds of the monastery singing from the psalms as he went. Benedicta Ward writes of 'the use of the psalter as the words through which someone could express his own prayer to Christ'.[25]

Out of his own use of the psalter, Bede composed an abbreviated psalter that became very influential in the history of prayer over the next four centuries. He selected a verse or verses from each psalm, verses that 'could be used as direct prayer or praise, as food for meditation, plea for mercy, protest, contrition, or adoration and exultation. The verses were also selected so that a sense of the meaning of the psalm as a whole was retained; it would be possible to recall the whole psalm from these clues.'[26] It was not only monks who used this short psalter; it was also used by hermits, some of whom had little education and would have been unable to recite the whole psalter, and by laymen as they went about their daily business.

Bede lived with the psalms; he also died with them. In his last illness he continued to teach, but would spend the rest of the day chanting the psalter, including the antiphons that pointed them towards Christ.

PRAYER

Gracious God, thank you for the foretaste of Christ in the psalms. As I read them and pray them, strengthen me in thanksgiving and in confession, and show me your mercy. Amen.

PRAYING THE PSALMS

Use one or more psalms each day this week in your prayers. You may already have favourites, but if you want some suggestions, these are the Lent psalms from The Daily Office SSF, the daily prayer book of my own community.

Sunday: Psalms 26; 86; 117
Monday: Psalms 32; 102; 150
Tuesday: Psalms 38; 56; 146
Wednesday: Psalms 3; 6; 90; 147:13–20
Thursday: Psalms 25; 27; 148
Friday: Psalms 39; 69; 147:1–12
Saturday: Psalms 13; 31; 124; 149

As you pray, look out for verses that particularly speak to you, and gather them in your own personal abbreviated psalter. You may want to continue with this practice throughout Lent, exploring more psalms and gathering more verses into your own psalter.

FINDING COMMUNITY

Bede lived nearly the whole of his life in the context of a particular kind of community. Where do you find community in your daily life? It may be in your family, in your church, in the workplace, in a political party or campaigning group, or through a shared sport, hobby or interest. What differences do you find between the community in groups that people have chosen to join, such as a club or workplace, and those that are more 'given', such as the family or church? How do you deal with difficulties and divisions when they arise? What would your ideal community look like? How can you help the communities in which you take part to come closer to that ideal?

LEARNING

What part does study—consciously setting out to learn—play in your Christian life? Do you share Bede's delight in it? Do you read only what you're comfortable with, that agrees with your views, or are you ready to be challenged and made uncomfortable by what you learn? If study and learning are not normally part of your life, try to make them so in this week. Find a book, video or website on something that interests you, and give yourself time to see what it has to teach you. If you are part of a group, you may recommend study material to each other.

One of my favourite quotations about learning is from *The Once and Future King*, the book about King Arthur by T.H. White.

'The best thing for being sad,' replied Merlyn, beginning to puff and blow, 'is to learn something. That is the only thing that never fails. You may grow old and trembling in your anatomies, you may lie awake at night, listening to the disorder of your veins, you may miss your only love, you may see the world about you devastated by evil lunatics or know your honour trampled in the sewers of baser minds. There is only one thing for it then—to learn. Learn why the world wags and what wags it. That is the only thing which the mind can never exhaust, never alienate, never be tortured by, never fear or distrust, and never dream of regretting.'[27]

Another aspect of learning is learning by heart. It may seem unnecessary now, when everyone has access to books, but stocking your mind with words from God can be a marvellous way of following Paul's injunction in Philippians 4:8: 'Finally, beloved, whatever is true, whatever is honourable, whatever is just, whatever is pure, whatever is pleasing, whatever is commendable, if there is any excellence and if there is anything worthy of praise, think about these things.'

Memorizing favourite Bible verses, prayers, hymns and poetry, gives you a stock of 'pure, pleasing, commendable' words to draw on anywhere at any time—while driving, queuing or in a waiting-room.

Aelred of Rievaulx

Sunday

MAN OF FRIENDSHIP

'This is my commandment, that you love one another as I have loved you. No one has greater love than this, to lay down one's life for one's friends. You are my friends if you do what I command you. I do not call you servants any longer, because the servant does not know what the master is doing; but I have called you friends, because I have made known to you everything that I have heard from my Father.'

JOHN 15:12–15

Friendship was the great theme of our next writer and guide, Aelred of Rievaulx. Aelred, like Bede, lived in the north of England, but several centuries later: he was born in 1110. There is another link with Bede, too. Aelred's great-grandfather, Alfred, was the treasurer of the Durham shrine of St Cuthbert, the great northern saint about whom Bede wrote two biographies. Alfred was also a priest at Hexham in Northumberland, as were Aelred's grandfather and father, and it was there that Aelred was born.

His family was well connected, and Aelred had a good education, some of it at the monastic school in Durham. At the age of 15 he was sent to the Scottish court of King David I to complete his education and begin his life of service. He was a friend of Henry, the king's heir, and of the king's stepsons, Simon and Waldef. He may have been steward of the royal household, a responsible position, and one requiring the gifts of administration that his later life demonstrated.

In 1134, aged 24, Aelred travelled south in the king's service to visit Walter Espec, Lord of Helmsley in north Yorkshire and patron of a new Cistercian monastery nearby at Rievaulx. Aelred visited the monastery briefly and, instead of travelling back to Scotland, returned the next day to join the community. He spent nearly the whole of the rest of his life there, including 20 years as abbot.

As we can see from this sudden turnaround in his life, Aelred was a man of strong feelings, and was not afraid to act on them. There were times when his powerful emotions and the relationships engendered by them caused him great anxiety, but feeling and friendship were also at the heart of his life as a Christian and a monk. They were central to his two best-known books, *The Mirror of Charity*, and *Spiritual Friendship*. Although the latter draws on many of the classical works on friendship, it goes beyond them. One commentator writes, 'Aelred's discussion of spiritual friendship is both clear on all points and original, discussing with great perception issues which had not been treated by his masters, Augustine and the other Fathers of the monastic tradition.'[1]

Because friendship was so important for Aelred, it was not to be entered into lightly. He describes the friend as 'the companion of your soul, to whose spirit you join and attach yours, and so associate yourself that you wish to become one instead of two' and as 'one to whom you entrust yourself as to another self, from whom you hide nothing, from whom you fear nothing'.[2]

The echoes with Jesus' words to his disciples in today's reading are clear. Jesus has made known to them everything he has heard from his Father, and he has specifically chosen them. I always find Mark 3:13 very moving in its simplicity: 'Jesus went up the mountain and called to him those whom he wanted, and they came to him.' These are the people to whom he will entrust his secrets, and who will become, after his death, his presence in the world— 'another self' indeed.

It might seem that Jesus was less wise than Aelred in those whom he chose to be his friends. Aelred recommends a slow process of increasing closeness, testing whether the potential friend has the qualities necessary to enter into true friendship. Jesus seems to have called in a moment and, despite misunderstandings (for example, the argument over precedence in Matthew 20:20–28), eventual betrayal and desertion, he never wavered in his love for his friends. It is, after all, at the Last Supper that he gives them the new commandment found in our reading for today, and calls them his friends.

It is to the love of Christ that all of Aelred's writing on friendship leads. Friendship has its own value, but its overriding purpose is to lead to Christ. Friendship with the seen and known brother or sister leads to friendship with the unseen Christ, who can be known through love. 'And thus, friend cleaving to friend in the spirit of Christ, is made with Christ but one heart and one soul.'[3]

PRAYER

Jesus, friend and saviour, make me day by day more truly your friend. Be yourself the companion of my soul, from whom I hide nothing, from whom I fear nothing, so that I may come to be one heart and one soul with you. Amen.

Monday

A BALANCED LIFE

Now as they went on their way, he entered a certain village, where a woman named Martha welcomed him into her home. She had a sister named Mary, who sat at the Lord's feet and listened to what he was saying. But Martha was distracted by her many tasks; so she came to him and asked, 'Lord, do you not care that my sister has left me to do all the work by myself? Tell her then to help me.' But the Lord answered her, 'Martha, Martha, you are worried and distracted by many things; there is need of only one thing. Mary has chosen the better part, which will not be taken away from her.'
LUKE 10:38–42

The 'certain village' is Bethany, a little way east of Jerusalem, and it was an important place of friendship for Jesus. It was the home of Martha, Mary and Lazarus. Jesus stayed in Bethany between his triumphal entry into Jerusalem on Palm Sunday and the contro-versial day that followed as the net began to close in on him (Matthew 21:17), and it was there, later in the week, that a woman anointed his head with ointment as he stayed with Simon the leper (Matthew 26:6–12). Perhaps another version of the same story is to be found in John 12:1–8; this time the setting is the home of Martha, Mary and Lazarus, and it is Mary who anoints Jesus' feet with ointment.

Aelred would have heard today's passage every year on 15 August, the feast of the Assumption. This was the patronal festival of the Cistercians, and the entire community, both monks and lay brothers (a total of 600 at Rievaulx by the time Aelred died), came together to celebrate. Many of Aelred's surviving sermons come from this festival day. He may well have used this story to illustrate his great theme of friendship.

In the household at Bethany there was an example of three distinct and different people living together, mainly in harmony, but (from the evidence of this story) experiencing some of the real struggles that we all face in our relationships with others. It was also a household that welcomed Jesus into its midst, which perhaps he needed as a place to escape the insistent demands of the crowds, to relax with people who knew him and loved him. In one of his sermons Aelred said, 'Almighty God could no doubt grant instant perfection to everyone and bestow all the virtues on each of us. But his loving arrangement is that we should need one another.'[4]

Is it too bold to suggest that in this household at Bethany, God, incarnate in Christ, experienced for himself this need for other people, for friends? There is an easy intimacy in the stories of Bethany that makes them powerful material for prayer, especially the imaginative style of prayer in which we put ourselves into the Gospel story.

There was also another way in which this particular story of Bethany was used by Aelred. One of his sermons for the feast of the Assumption uses it to explore the relationship between the active and the contemplative lives, between work and prayer. And although the story has often been used to promote the superiority of the contemplative, of Mary's 'better part', Aelred takes a more balanced view. 'Both of these women,' he tells his brothers, 'are in the one house, both are pleasing and acceptable to the Lord, both are loved by the Lord'[5] and 'Never in this life should these two women be separated.'[6] Drawing on Christ's great teaching on the last judgment in Matthew 25:31–46, he speaks of the need for practical works of service, because in the guise of his brothers and sisters, Christ is still 'hungry and thirsty and is tempted'.[7] Martha's work is right and necessary, but it is also right to sit at Jesus' feet and learn from him, as Mary did.

By no means should you neglect Mary for the sake of Martha, nor again Martha for the sake of Mary. For if you neglect Martha, who will feed Jesus? If you neglect Mary, what benefit will it be to you that Jesus entered your house since you have not tasted anything of his sweetness?[8]

And so his brothers were to do everything in its proper time, neglecting neither prayer for the sake of practical work nor practical work for the sake of prayer. This balance was to be found in the life of each individual brother: it was not right that some should be all Martha and others all Mary.

Jesus' words about Mary's 'better part' should cheer us, Aelred says, because they assure us that Martha's labours will end with our earthly life, but Mary's contemplation of God will not.

Mary's part will not be taken away from us, rather it will be increased. What here we begin to taste in some tiny drops, after this life we will drink until we enjoy a certain spiritual inebriation... Let us yearn hungrily for a taste of the divine sweetness, for here indeed it begins, but after this life it will reach its perfection in us and remain with us for all eternity.[9]

PRAYER

Jesus, may I make of my heart and soul a Bethany for you, a place of friendship, of service, and of contemplation of you. Give me now a taste of the sweetness of loving you which will come to perfection in heaven. Amen.

Tuesday

MIRACLE AT BETHANY

Now a certain man was ill, Lazarus of Bethany, the village of Mary and her sister Martha... So the sisters sent a message to Jesus, 'Lord, he whom you love is ill.' ...

When Jesus arrived, he found that Lazarus had already been in the tomb for four days... When Martha heard that Jesus was coming, she went and met him, while Mary stayed at home. Martha said to Jesus, 'Lord, if you had been here, my brother would not have died. But even now I know that God will give you whatever you ask of him.' Jesus said to her, 'Your brother will rise again.' Martha said to him, 'I know that he will rise again in the resurrection on the last day.' Jesus said to her, 'I am the resurrection and the life. Those who believe in me, even though they die, will live, and everyone who lives and believes in me will never die. Do you believe this?' She said to him, 'Yes, Lord, I believe that you are the Messiah, the Son of God, the one coming into the world.'

JOHN 11:1, 3, 17, 20–27

This is the longest and perhaps the most vivid of all the stories of Jesus and his friends at Bethany. There isn't space to print it all here, but you might like to read the entire story (John 11:1–44). It is a beautifully written and dramatic story with many twists and turns, as Jesus, apparently uncaring, waits several days before going to Bethany in response to the message of Mary and Martha. There is the perplexity of the disciples, along with their determination to stick with their friend Jesus even when they don't understand what he's doing. There is Martha's rebuke to Jesus—'Lord, if you had been here, my brother would not have died'—and the profound dialogue that follows, in which Jesus draws out her faith to produce the great statement, 'Yes, Lord, I believe that you are the Messiah, the Son of God', a parallel to Peter's confession of faith at Caesarea Philippi (Matthew 16:13–20).

Continuing from the part of the story printed here is, of course, the raising of Lazarus, with Jesus' sharing in the grief of his friends, weeping with them, before commanding Lazarus to come out of his tomb.

The home at Bethany is the scene of one of Jesus' greatest miracles, one that shows him to be truly God, while at the same time showing him as most truly human in his grief. Aelred found comfort in this part of the story in his own time of grief, after the death of a dear friend and fellow monk, Simon. He wrote a passionate eulogy for him, which he included in *The Mirror of Charity*. In it he is very frank about his sorrow.

Grief prevents me from going further. The recent death of my dear Simon forcibly drives me instead to weep for him… You are astonished that I am weeping. You are still more astonished that I go on living! For who would not be astonished that Aelred goes on living without Simon, except someone who does not know how sweet it was to live together, how sweet it would be to return together to the fatherland. So bear patiently with my tears, my sighs, the moaning of my heart, then.[10]

In his bereavement, however, he finds comfort in the memory of Jesus' tears for his friend Lazarus: 'Yet the tears you shed over the death of your friend excuse us, Lord, for they express our affection and give us a glimpse of your charity… Oh, how sweet are your tears and how gentle. What savour and consolation they give to my troubled mind.'[11]

The friendship of Jesus with Mary, Martha and Lazarus is the context in this Gospel story for many great things, both in teaching and in action. Aelred, along with other Cistercians, would have been drawn to it by its depth of feeling. A new valuing of feeling, of affectivity, was one of the great gifts of the Cistercians to their fellow Christians, both then and now. They picked up and applied to their faith a revolution in relationships in the society of their day, a revolution embodied in the notion of 'courtly love' and in the songs of the troubadours. The troubadours sang for the lady they loved, often from a distance; the monks sang of their love, ultimately for God, but also for those whose love and friendship were an important part of the journey to God. Unlike many earlier writers, they saw no need to shun human company in order to find God. In fact, they believed that concern and care for a friend could draw people closer to God.

And thus a friend praying to Christ on behalf of his friend, and for his friend's sake desiring to be heard by Christ, directs his attention with love and longing to Christ; then it sometimes happens that quickly and imperceptibly the one love passes over into the other, and coming, as it were, into close contact with the sweetness of Christ himself, the friend begins to taste his sweetness and to experience his charm.[12]

Surely this is a description of Martha's encounter with Christ, in which her love for her brother leads her into a deeper knowledge of the reality of Christ and into a confession of faith that makes her worthy, along with Mary Magdalene, first witness of the resurrection, to stand in the company of the apostles.

PRAYER

God of love, thank you for friendship, for those who walk with me on the journey of faith. In my love of them, may I draw nearer to you, and in my love of you, may I deepen my friendship with them. Amen.

Wednesday

CHRIST IN OUR MIDST

Now while Jesus was at Bethany in the house of Simon the leper, a woman came to him with an alabaster jar of very costly ointment, and she poured it on his head as he sat at the table. But when the disciples saw it, they were angry and said, 'Why this waste? For this ointment could have been sold for a large sum, and the money given to the poor.' But Jesus, aware of this, said to them, 'Why do you trouble the woman? She has performed a good service for me. For you always have the poor with you, but you will not always have me. By pouring this ointment on my body she has prepared me for burial. Truly I tell you, wherever this good news is proclaimed in the whole world, what she has done will be told in remembrance of her.'

MATTHEW 26:6–13

At the very beginning of Aelred's book, *Spiritual Friendship*, Christ is central. The book is written in the form of a dialogue between Aelred and several of his friends: Ivo, Walter and Gratian. It begins with Aelred saying to Ivo, 'Here we are, you and I, and I hope a third, Christ, is in our midst.'[13]

Aelred's emphasis on human friendship did not lessen the importance, indeed the centrality, of Christ. Ivo is soon asking, 'I should like also to be instructed more fully as to how the friendship which ought to exist among us begins in Christ, is preserved according to the Spirit of Christ, and how its end and fruition are referred to Christ.'[14]

Christ is, of course, at the centre of all the Bethany stories. Traditionally, the woman in this story of Bethany has been identified with Mary Magdalene, and with Mary the sister of Martha. Scholars now separate the various 'Marys' in the Gospel stories, and this is probably more accurate. But there is still something powerful about looking at the stories together. They show us a picture of a passionate woman who is not afraid to demonstrate her love of Christ publicly—anointing his head and his feet, sitting at his feet in the traditional place of a male disciple of a rabbi. She is not afraid of his physicality; indeed, others are embarrassed and outraged by her extravagant love.

She shows us how Christ's disciples are called to serve his body—not now his physical body, but his body in the church and the world. Christ is still present in the poor and the suffering, and his body can be honoured when they are served and honoured.

Aelred, characteristically, writes of the centrality of Christ in language full of feeling. He speaks of how he was drawn from secular learning to the scriptures, until he wanted to read only what 'had been sweetened by the honey of the most sweet name of Jesus'.[15] He is very creative in the titles by which he addresses Jesus and the biblical images he uses about him. A few of these titles give a flavour of his thought: Jesus is our Physician, the Wisdom of God, the Poor One, Strength, Light, the Author of Creation, the Lord of the Angels. His many images also bring out different facets of Christ: he is cloud, a bracelet, the ark, the keystone, the sweetest of grapes, emperor, a mountain.[16] Christ is at the heart of Aelred's faith, and appears in every one of the sermons he preached at Rievaulx.

'He alone in all,' he writes in *The Mirror of Charity*, 'he alone above all, both captures our attachment and demands our love. He claims for himself a place in the abode of our heart, not only the most important place but the highest; not only the highest but also the innermost.'[17]

One way of allowing Jesus to have his place in the heart was to meditate on the Gospel stories. Aelred taught this way of prayer especially in a book written for his sister, who was living a solitary life. He gives her models of imaginative meditation for many Gospel stories, from the annunciation to the resurrection, models in which she 'enters into the scenes she is contemplating, following the characters about, sympathizing with their feelings and reactions, and making their situations her own, so that their life becomes hers'.[18] The aim of such prayer, as of the friendship that he values so highly, is to bring the Christian into unity of spirit with Christ: 'mounting aloft through degrees of love to friendship with Christ, he is made one spirit with him in one kiss'.[19]

The passionate nature of such an encounter with Christ is beautifully captured in his meditation on another of the anointing stories (Luke 7:36–50):

Now go into the Pharisee's house and see our Lord in his place at table there. Together with that most blessed sinner approach his feet, wash them with your tears, wipe them with your hair, soothe them with kisses and warm them with ointments. Are you not already penetrated with the fragrance of that sacred oil? If he still will not let you approach his feet, be insistent, beseech him, raise your eyes to him brimming with tears and extort from him with deep sighs and unutterable groanings what you seek.[20]

PRAYER

Beloved Jesus, come and dwell in my heart, take captive all my desires, and let all my love be focused on you. Be yourself the beginning and the end of all my activity, until I am at last united with you in one spirit. Amen.

Thursday

THE CONSOLATIONS OF SCRIPTURE

Now Isaac had come from Beer-lahai-roi, and was settled in the
Negeb. Isaac went out in the evening to walk in the field; and
looking up, he saw camels coming. And Rebekah looked up, and
when she saw Isaac, she slipped quickly from the camel, and said
to the servant, 'Who is the man over there, walking in the field to
meet us?' The servant said, 'It is my master.' So she took her veil
and covered herself. And the servant told Isaac all the things that
he had done. Then Isaac brought her into his mother Sarah's tent.
He took Rebekah, and she became his wife; and he loved her. So
Isaac was comforted after his mother's death.

GENESIS 24:62–67

We saw yesterday how Aelred was wooed from his love of secular
literature to love only that which contained 'the most sweet name
of Jesus'.[21] In fact, it was not only the New Testament that drew him,
but all of the scriptures. It is hard to imagine how central the Bible
was to Christians of Aelred's time, and especially to monks. Other
books were scarce and expensive, and monastic common prayer
was almost entirely made up of scripture, in particular the psalms.
So it is not surprising that when they came to write, they did so,
as one writer beautifully puts it, 'with pens dipped in the ink of
Scripture'.[22] Their language and imagery are shaped by biblical
language and imagery to such an extent that it is often hard to know
when they are quoting directly from the Bible and when they are
not. With even Bibles scarce, they were often quoting from memory,

and therefore not always accurately, but it rarely matters. If their books are 'a tapestry of biblical texts',[23] they are beautiful and inspiring tapestries.

Aelred uses this passage, which might seem quite unpromising at first sight, as the inspiration for a beautiful meditation on 'the consolations of scripture'.

Brethren, however cast down we may be by harassment or heartache, the consolations of Scripture will lift us up again... This is the field where Isaac walked in the evening meditating, and where Rebecca came hurrying towards him and soothed with her gentle charm the grief that had befallen him. How often, good Jesus, does day incline to evening, how often does the daylight of some slight consolation fade before the black night of an intolerable grief? Everything turns to ashes in my mouth; wherever I look, I see a load of cares. If someone speaks to me, I barely hear; if someone knocks, I scarcely notice; my heart is turned to stone, my tongue sticks fast, my tear-ducts are dry. What then? Into the field I go to meditate. I reread the holy book; I set down my thoughts; and suddenly Rebecca comes running towards me and with her light, which is your grace, good Jesus, dispels the gloom, puts melancholy to flight, disintegrates my hardness. Soon sighs give way to tears, accompanied in their turn by heavenly joy. Unhappy are those who, when oppressed in spirit, do not walk into this field and find that joy.[24]

This is a good example of the way in which monks read the scriptures. Their primary interest was not intellectual or theological, but spiritual. They read in order to find God. Aelred often preached on this subject, speaking of the scriptures as 'the gateway to that personal experience of God in every life, which establishes a personal bond that temptation and difficulty cannot break'.[25] He uses images from the scriptures to illustrate his point: 'The scriptures are the star that leads us to Jesus, the tomb we must approach like the women on the morning of the resurrection, expectantly carrying our spices of faith, devotion, and love.'[26]

Even when Jesus is not directly present in the text, as in the Old

Testament, these readers found him, following the biblical writers themselves in seeing the Old Testament as foreshadowing and prophesying Christ's coming. As one writer puts it, 'Where they found the Old Testament abstruse, they approached it obliquely by means of allegory and surprised it into rendering a meaning.'[27]

They were also capable of great simplicity. Aelred uses the delightful image of himself as a puppy.

Good Jesus, be present! Be present to this little pauper of yours who is… begging… like a puppy, for those crumbs which fall from the table of my masters, your sons… Since the puppies eat the crumbs which fall from their masters' tables, break some of that bread up for your puppy, so that someone who cannot manage to eat the crust may gather up the crumbs.[28]

From the deepest realms of prayer to the simplest and most homely of images, scripture shaped and informed the lives of Aelred and his fellow monks in a way very difficult to recapture today. But perhaps we too can choose to step into the field and find there the light and grace of Jesus.

PRAYER

Jesus, Word of God, give me today a fresh enthusiasm for the scriptures. Send me your light and your grace as I read; break open the tomb as I come with my faith, devotion and love; lead me through all that I read and ponder to you. Amen.

Friday

MARY OUR MOTHER

Now every year Jesus' parents went to Jerusalem for the festival of the Passover. And when he was twelve years old, they went up as usual for the festival. When the festival was ended and they started to return, the boy Jesus stayed behind in Jerusalem, but his parents did not know it. Assuming that he was in the group of travellers, they went a day's journey. Then they started to look for him among their relatives and friends. When they did not find him, they returned to Jerusalem to search for him. After three days they found him in the temple, sitting among the teachers, listening to them and asking them questions. And all who heard him were amazed at his understanding and his answers. When his parents saw him they were astonished; and his mother said to him, 'Child, why have you treated us like this? Look, your father and I have been searching for you in great anxiety.' He said to them, 'Why were you searching for me? Did you not know that I must be in my Father's house?' But they did not understand what he said to them. Then he went down with them and came to Nazareth, and was obedient to them. His mother treasured all these things in her heart.

LUKE 2:41–51

This is a story that Aelred knew very well. He wrote a short book on it, a work at once theological and devotional. He encourages his readers to use their imagination to enter into the story. 'Where were you those three days, good Jesus? Who set food and drink before you? Who made your bed? Who took your shoes off?'[29]

The questions are those that any mother would ask herself about a missing child. As both a Cistercian and a man of the twelfth century, Aelred would have had a particular devotion to Mary, the mother of Jesus. Bernard of Clairvaux, the founder of the Cistercians, was a leader in a new movement of feeling for the humanity and suffering of Christ, which brought with it a new devotion to his mother, through whom he received his humanity and who suffered with him.

In one of his many sermons on the Assumption, a feast celebrating the death of Mary and her triumphant reception into heaven, Aelred shows her as always seeking Jesus.

See, brothers, and, if you can, conceive and picture to yourselves how the blessed Mary felt in regard to her dearest Son today, to what glory she came, how perfectly the love and knowledge of his divinity absorbed her. That is why she says that up to this time she did not find him, even though she gave birth to him from the womb. This we have said of her first seeking. She sought him again through his passion, after his death. This was a quest full of sorrow and anxiety.[30]

In this lifetime of seeking, Mary is perhaps being presented as a model for the monk, who has left everything else in order to seek God. But of course, in the end, this is the call to all Christians; to place the search for God above all else. Sometimes this will be a cause of joy for us, sometimes of 'great anxiety', but we can be sure (although it will not always feel like this) that those who truly seek will find.

In another way, too, Aelred presents Mary as a model, first for his monks and then for everyone. Referring to the Gospel writer's words, 'They did not understand what he said to them', Aelred reflects that, full of the Holy Spirit as Mary was, she could not have been ignorant of her son's purpose. Instead, she 'treasured all these things in her heart', and Aelred presents a marvellous picture of Mary remembering all that Jesus did, and meditating on it, for the sake of the Gospel writers and their readers.

So the most blessed Virgin was even then making merciful provision for us, in order that matters so sweet, so wholesome, so necessary, might not be lost to memory through any neglect... then when the time came [she] told of them and entrusted them to the holy apostles and disciples to be preached.[31]

Perhaps unusually for a man of his time, Aelred wrote of men and women as equals, using the story of the creation of woman in Genesis 2:21–22 to say, 'How beautiful it is that the second human being was taken from the side of the first, so that nature might teach that human beings are equal.'[32] So he was able also to identify himself with Mary as a model of discipleship. When predicting his death, he referred to his soul, in the words of the Magnificat, which he would have sung every day at Vespers, as 'the handmaid of the Lord'.

Always, though, devotion to Mary is because of her relationship with Christ. Because she is Christ's mother, and Aelred is seeking to be more and more closely identified with Christ, Mary is his mother too: 'Our true birth is of her' and 'through her comes... our rearing, our growth.'[33] For many of us, this may be a new idea, but it may be a fruitful one as we ponder this story of losing and finding.

PRAYER

Jesus, son of Mary, may the heart of your mother be mine today as I seek to follow the will of your Father and mine; and may I, with her, treasure all your words and deeds in my heart. Amen.

Saturday

KEEPING THE SABBATH

If you remove the yoke from among you, the pointing of the finger, the speaking of evil, if you offer your food to the hungry and satisfy the needs of the afflicted, then your light shall rise in the darkness and your gloom be like the noonday. The Lord will guide you continually, and satisfy your needs in parched places, and make your bones strong; and you shall be like a watered garden, like a spring of water, whose waters never fail...

If you refrain from trampling the sabbath, from pursuing your own interests on my holy day; if you call the sabbath a delight and the holy day of the Lord honourable; if you honour it, not going your own ways, serving your own interests, or pursuing your own affairs; then you shall take delight in the Lord, and I will make you ride upon the heights of the earth; I will feed you with the heritage of your ancestor Jacob, for the mouth of the Lord has spoken.

ISAIAH 58:9B–11, 13–14

Aelred wrote in *Spiritual Friendship*:

The day before yesterday, as I was walking the round of the cloister of the monastery, the brethren were sitting around forming as it were a most loving crown. In the midst, as it were, of the delights of paradise with the leaves, flowers and fruits of each single tree, I marvelled. In that multitude of brethren I found no one whom I did not love and no one by whom, I felt sure, I was not loved.[34]

I am willing to believe that Aelred, with his intense emotional responses to life, did feel like this on occasion, and did indeed find his life in the monastery a foretaste of heaven. But I'm also well aware from my own experience of community life that it isn't always like that.

The sabbath itself was intended as a foretaste of the life of heaven, and, thinking back to the story of Mary and Martha, we can perhaps see why it came to be kept as a day free from work and devoted to prayer and worship. Although the sabbath could be perverted into a joyless day on which even playing with toys was forbidden, at root it was a positive impulse.

Aelred uses the image of the sabbath extensively, especially in *The Mirror of Charity*. It 'takes its origin in God's sabbath, God's rest on the seventh day as recorded in Genesis. God's rest is the source of our rest and our peace, and it is also our goal'.[35] Before we reach this sabbath of sabbaths, though, there are two others that pave the way. The first sabbath is love of self, the second love of neighbour. They are not really separate, but facets of the same love: 'these three loves are engendered by one another, nourished by one another, and fanned into flame by one another. Then they are all brought to perfection together.'[36]

We can easily see how friendship fits here, as part of the love of neighbour. Indeed, Aelred sees friendship as having something of eternity about it: 'was it not a foretaste of blessedness thus to love and thus to be loved?' he asks, writing of one of his closest friends.[37]

The 'rest' of the sabbath, of heaven, was not something that Aelred experienced often in this life. As abbot of a large and growing monastery, much of his time was taken up with administrative duties and the pastoral care of his monks. Rievaulx had four daughter houses in England and Scotland, and Aelred visited them regularly, also attending annual meetings of the General Chapter of the order at Citeaux in France. Other church business took him at least once to Rome, and all over England.

Some of this travelling was curtailed by poor health; for half of his 20 years as abbot his health was so bad that the Rule had to be modified for him. Sickness often makes us weary of others, but Aelred did not withdraw from those around him. He had a small room near the infirmary, where sick monks were cared for, where he could have a fire in the cold days of the Yorkshire winter. The other monks would come, 20 or 30 at a time, to talk to him, and he seems never to have turned them away.

In the last year of his life, further illness afflicted him, until by Christmas 1166 he was praying for death. Early in January, he gathered all the monks together and said, 'I am going home from exile, out of darkness into light.'[38] He continued to pray and to have the scriptures read to him, and his monks and fellow abbots gathered around him. Aelred died on 12 January 1167, surrounded by his friends, and going to his greatest friend, the Christ to whom he had given his life.

PRAYER

Jesus, friend and saviour, thank you for Aelred of Rievaulx, for his humanity and his passion for you. Bring me, like him, to a perfect trust in you and in your purposes for me, so that I may come at the end of my life to share in your eternal rest, to the sabbath of sabbaths in heaven. Amen.

< Performance >

MEDITATING ON SCRIPTURE

Follow Aelred's example in meditating imaginatively on Bible stories, especially those of Jesus. You may like to focus particularly on the stories set in Bethany. Allow your feelings to be engaged as you enter into the stories. You may already have your own way of doing this, but if it is a new idea to you, here is an example based on the story of Mary and Martha, which we used on Monday.

Read the biblical story through twice, slowly. If you are in a group, ask two different members to read it, with a short pause in between. It's best if they read from the same version: this is prayer, not Bible study, and it is better not to be distracted by interesting variations in the translation. Allow yourself/each other a little time to settle into a comfortable, prayerful position, and to commend the time to God.

If you're in a group, you might ask one member to read the following suggestions slowly, allowing plenty of space in between for individuals to enter into the story. If you're the one leading, allow a bit more time than feels comfortable to you, and you'll probably be setting the right pace. If you're doing this exercise on your own, just use the suggestions at your own pace.

You are standing outside the home of Martha, Mary and Lazarus ...... What can you see... hear... feel... smell... touch? How do you feel? ...... Open the door and enter the house ...... Who else is there? ...... What are they doing? ...... You are someone who feels at home here, so where do you settle? ...... Are you with Martha in the kitchen, with Mary at Jesus' feet, or somewhere else? ...... Are you comfortable in your place, or would you rather be somewhere else? ...... Can you hear Jesus talking? ...... What is he saying? ...... How do you answer? ...... Allow the conversation to continue for a time ...... or perhaps you just want to be with Jesus, silently ...... It is time to leave, so draw your time with Jesus to a close ...... and say goodbye for the present.

Allow yourself/each other a little time to come back to the here and now. This kind of prayer can be very powerful, and sometimes unexpected things happen. You may want to share something of your prayer with each other, or with a spiritual friend.

CELEBRATING JESUS

Aelred used many different ways of describing and naming Jesus; some of them were given in Wednesday's reflection. Try to compose your own 'litany' of names of Jesus. This can be an exercise in knowing and using the Bible, as you seek out the names and images that the biblical writers apply to Jesus, and put them together in a litany form. Here are some examples using Aelred's titles:

Jesus, Physician, heal me of all my wounds and sickness;
Jesus, Wisdom of God, enlighten me with your words and example;
Jesus, Author of Creation, help me to see your hand in all your works.

Alternatively, you may do this exercise in a more personal way, noticing and using those images that particularly speak to you. Some will undoubtedly be from the Bible, but others may be from hymns and songs, or favourite spiritual writers. Begin to make a list now, and when you have a good number, use your creativity to draw them together into prayers for your own use. If you are really inspired, you may also find visual images that speak to you of Jesus or illustrate some of the titles and images you've found. You could use them to create your own small prayer book.

REFLECTING ON FRIENDSHIP

Aelred described a friend as someone 'to whom we can fearlessly entrust our heart and all its secrets'. How important is friendship in your life? Do you set out to find friends, make efforts to grow together, and become people who can 'fearlessly entrust your hearts' to each other? What have you learnt from friendship, which you can apply to your relationship with God?

What are your first memories of friendship? Most of us will have had very intense childhood friendships at some time. Are these happy memories for you, or are they tinged with regret, sorrow or pain? If healing is needed, bring these memories into prayer, or talk them through with someone you trust.

Is the description of Jesus as 'friend' one that feels comfortable to you? You may like to re-read Jesus' words in our Sunday reading and, in a time of prayer, hear him saying these words to you individually. You may want to hear him using your name, saying, '............ , I call you my friend.' How do you feel in doing this? If you really thought of Jesus as the best friend you have ever experienced or could imagine, how might it change your relationship with him?

The Cloud of Unknowing

INTO THE CLOUD

Then came the day of Unleavened Bread, on which the Passover lamb had to be sacrificed. So Jesus sent Peter and John, saying, 'Go and prepare the Passover meal for us that we may eat it.' They asked him, 'Where do you want us to make preparations for it?' 'Listen,' he said to them, 'when you have entered the city, a man carrying a jar of water will meet you; follow him into the house he enters, and say to the owner of the house, "The teacher asks you, 'Where is the guest room, where I may eat the Passover with my disciples?'" He will show you a large room upstairs, already furnished. Make preparations for us there.' So they went and found everything as he had told them; and they prepared the Passover meal.

LUKE 22:7–13

This week's author is as anonymous as the man carrying the jar of water but, like the man with the jar and many of the other un-named figures in the Gospels, what he did has survived. The man in the Gospel played a small but crucial part in Jesus' celebration of the Passover with his disciples. Our companion this week wrote powerfully and originally on prayer.

It is from the title of the most substantial of his writings, *The Cloud of Unknowing*, that he gets his 'name': the *Cloud* author. One of the few things about this author that seems almost certain is that he was male. All the evidence points to his having been a priest, and in the 14th century, that meant he was a man. In the final paragraph of *The Cloud of Unknowing*, he gives 'God's blessing and mine' to his reader. But there are many opinions about what kind of priest he was—a parish priest, a member of a religious community, active or enclosed, a hermit or a recluse. From the English he uses, it is generally agreed that he lived and worked in the East Midlands.

The personal note of that final paragraph and its blessing are characteristic of all of this author's writings. Most seem to have been written to a particular person, aged 24 when *The Cloud* was written, whom the author was guiding in a life of prayer. This relationship was a long-term one, as at least two of the author's later writings, *The Epistle of Privy Counsel* and *The Epistle of Prayer*, are addressed to the same disciple, answering questions and difficulties that he has raised.

Despite the demanding and austere nature of the spiritual journey that the author describes to his disciple, their relationship was warm and affectionate. The disciple is addressed as 'my friend in God', and the author at one point protests that he is prompted by love in his rebuke to his disciple. At the beginning of *The Epistle of Privy Counsel*, he writes, 'If I understand your mind aright, as I think I do, I am going to speak to you personally, and not to any of those who may chance to overhear',[1] and at the end of *The Epistle of Prayer* he hopes that what he has suggested will 'be a real help to you, and not too unsuited to your make-up'.[2]

Many of Jesus' encounters, with the named and the unnamed, are marked by this same personal concern and knowledge. He treats those he meets as individuals, not simply as yet another person making demands upon him.

We are fortunate that the works of the *Cloud* author, written for a particular person, have survived and can speak to us today. They were written in the second half of the 14th century, but one of the most important influences on them was an anonymous Syrian monk of the late fifth or early sixth century, who took the pseudonym of Dionysius of Athens (a man converted by Paul in Acts 17:34). The *Cloud* author made a translation of this monk's best-known work, *The Mystical Theology*. In this short work, Dionysius writes of coming to God by way of darkness and unknowing, moving beyond what the mind can know and into the mystery of God. But although the *Cloud* author sees the need for this darkness and unknowing (indeed, taking Dionysius' phrase 'the darkness of unknowing' and making it 'the cloud of unknowing' and the title of his major work), he goes beyond this point. Where Dionysius saw union with God taking place when reason was exhausted, the *Cloud* author saw affection replacing reason. In one of his most famous sentences, he says, 'By love [God] can be caught and held, but by thinking never.'[3]

It is this stress on love as the ultimate means of knowing God that gives his works their warmth. They are not simple; one author says, 'The subject matter of the Cloud is admittedly difficult, and its practice even more so',[4] but the author's desire to draw his young disciple deeper into the life of prayer, and the images he uses in doing so, are very attractive and encourage the reader to persevere.

PRAYER

God of love, lead me to know you more by love. Amen.

Monday

GOD'S GIFT OF PRAYER

Then the word of the Lord came to him, saying, 'What are you doing here, Elijah?' He answered, 'I have been very zealous for the Lord, the God of hosts; for the Israelites have forsaken your covenant, thrown down your altars, and killed your prophets with the sword. I alone am left, and they are seeking my life, to take it away.'

He said, 'Go out and stand on the mountain before the Lord, for the Lord is about to pass by.' Now there was a great wind, so strong that it was splitting mountains and breaking rocks in pieces before the Lord, but the Lord was not in the wind; and after the wind an earthquake, but the Lord was not in the earthquake; and after the earthquake a fire, but the Lord was not in the fire; and after the fire a sound of sheer silence. When Elijah heard it, he wrapped his face in his mantle and went out and stood at the entrance of the cave. Then there came a voice to him that said, 'What are you doing here, Elijah?'

1 KINGS 19:9B–13

Elijah has been very active in God's service, and has suffered hardship because of it. He had perhaps created his own fire and earthquake and great wind—had been noticed and influential. But now God is calling him to something different, to find him in 'sheer silence'.

This is a vivid picture of the setting of *The Cloud of Unknowing*. It is addressed to someone whose way of knowing God is changing.

He has been actively engaged in God's service, working to serve him better in his world and to abandon all that is sinful. His prayer has engaged all his faculties—his mind, feelings and imagination. But now, perhaps to his puzzlement, these things no longer draw or hold him. Instead he feels called to the darkness of contemplation, going beyond where his human faculties can take him and into the cloud of unknowing.

This movement is in accordance with traditional understandings of the development of prayer, although today we would perhaps see the various stages as less of a ladder and more of a spiral. As our life progresses, we move from one stage to another, at times going forward and at other times returning to somewhere we have already been, but bringing with us the fruits of our time in another kind of prayer. Prayer is not a competitive sport, and it is important that we pray as we are being led by God now, rather than trying to follow a pattern of development laid down by someone else.

The *Cloud* author addresses those at a particular place on the spiral of prayer, who are being drawn away from a discursive type of meditation, filled with images, and towards the prayer of quiet, of simply being with God. In this prayer, thought has no place. 'Put speculation firmly aside,' the author writes, 'and worship God with all that you have. All-that-you-are-as-you-are worshipping all-that-he-is-as-he-is.'[5]

This is not a call for everyone, and the *Cloud* author gives considerable space in his various works to ways of knowing whether one is being called to it. He is realistic. 'I would like to make it clear that not everyone who reads this book (or hears it read) and finds it pleasantly interesting is therefore called to contemplation. The inner excitement he feels may be not so much the attraction of grace as the arousal of natural curiosity.'[6]

But if there is a persistent desire in times of prayer for God himself, rather than for God's gifts or for looking at oneself or reflecting on the life of Christ, and also an unquenchable pleasure in the thought of this contemplative prayer—not just when actually hearing or reading about it, but a pleasure and desire that 'follows you around all day whatever you are doing, interferes with your customary daily prayers, intruding between them and you'[7]—then this is a real call into a new way of prayer.

It is not a reward for good behaviour, but a gift of God, 'and it is not given for innocence or *withheld* for sin'.[8] Neither is the felt desire for it constant; often it is withdrawn for a time, perhaps just to make it clear that this is a gift and not something earned by hard work or kept by diligence.

For those called to this prayer, who answer the call and engage in it with their whole selves, everything else will fall into place. Food and drink, sleep, how to allocate times for prayer, reading, work, relationships with others ('If only I might always be preoccupied and faithful to the work of love in my heart!'[9]), all of these will find their rightful place.

We may be reminded of Elijah, whose needs for food and drink were met as he journeyed into the wilderness to encounter God (1 Kings 19:4–8), and of Jesus' words, 'And do not keep striving for what you are to eat and what you are to drink… Instead, strive for his kingdom, and these things will be given to you as well' (Luke 12:29, 31).

PRAYER

Gracious God, help me to see clearly the gift of prayer that you hold out to me now, and to embrace it wholeheartedly. Amen.

Tuesday

A NAKED INTENTION TO GOD

'Beware of practising your piety before others in order to be seen by them; for then you have no reward from your Father in heaven. So whenever you give alms, do not sound a trumpet before you, as the hypocrites do in the synagogues and in the streets, so that they may be praised by others. Truly I tell you, they have received their reward…

'And whenever you pray, do not be like the hypocrites; for they love to stand and pray in the synagogues and at the street corners, so that they may be seen by others. Truly I tell you, they have received their reward. But whenever you pray, go into your room and shut the door and pray to your Father who is in secret; and your Father who sees in secret will reward you.'

MATTHEW 6:1–2, 5–6

Jesus was realistic about the ways we can go astray in our prayer; and our human desire to be well thought of by others is just one of them. The *Cloud* author was equally down to earth about this, speaking from his own experience and probably from the experience of guiding others.

It is time to look a little more closely at the kind of prayer our companion is teaching. Jesus' words, 'Go into your room and shut the door and pray to your Father who is in secret' are a good starting point. The room doesn't have to be a physical one, but there is a call to withdraw from 'the synagogues and the street corners', and to shut out all that could come between God and the one who is praying. This includes good thoughts as much as bad ones, and even thinking about God and his wonderful works. There is a time for these thoughts, but the one called to contemplative prayer must leave them behind. Instead, there must be what the author calls 'a naked intention toward God, the desire for him alone'.[10]

He recommends that his disciple choose a short word to sum up his intention, and suggests 'God' or 'love'. Whenever a thought comes during the time of prayer, the disciple is to use the word to return to his intention. It is summed up in one short instruction: 'Lift your heart up to the Lord, with a gentle stirring of love desiring him for his own sake and not for his gifts.'[11]

As Jesus' warnings about how not to pray can help to clarify how we are to pray, so it is with the *Cloud* author's vivid descriptions of what can go wrong. It is possible to be truly called to this kind of prayer but to rush at it, trying to go too far too fast: 'Rely more on joyful enthusiasm than on sheer brute force.'[12] Then he has a lovely image: 'Learn to love joyfully with a sweet and gentle disposition of body and soul. Wait with gracious and modest courtesy for the Lord's initiative and do not impatiently snatch at grace like a greedy greyhound suffering from starvation.'[13]

Something else that we might want to snatch at is the consolation of prayer—feelings of sweetness and happiness, or of tears—but the *Cloud* author recommends sitting lightly to them. 'If they come, welcome them; but do not depend on them.'[14] The temptation is always to desire the consolations rather than the God who gives them. The author acknowledges, however, that some people need more consolation in their prayer than others—a good example of his respect for the individual and for the individual's way to God.

Taking things literally is another danger. As it would be foolish to take Jesus' words to mean that it is only possible to pray in a room of one's own, with the door closed, so the beginner contemplative, hearing others talk about going 'in' or 'up' in order to find God, may take this idea literally, confuse the physical and the spiritual, and strain his or her senses 'as though by brute force he could make his eyes and ears see and hear interior things'.[15] This wrong-headed contemplation leads to strange outward behaviour. 'Sometimes their eyes look like the eyes of wounded sheep near death. Some will let their heads droop to one side, as if a worm were in their ears... Others can neither sit, stand, nor lie down without moving their feet or gesturing with their hands.'[16]

This is a most unattractive picture! In contrast, true contemplation, engaged in by those truly called, seeking only God's will and not the good opinion or praise of others, has a 'good effect on the body as well as on the soul, for it makes them attractive in the eyes of all who see them'.[17]

PRAYER

God of love, you have planted the desire for you in my heart. Let my prayer be a response to this desire, and a simple expression of it. Keep me from the snares and delusions that can trip me up. Lead me into the room of my heart and help me to shut the door on all that holds me back from following you. Amen.

Wednesday

THE SINFUL SELF

This is the message we have heard from him and proclaim to you, that God is light and in him there is no darkness at all. If we say that we have fellowship with him while we are walking in darkness, we lie and do not do what is true; but if we walk in the light as he himself is in the light, we have fellowship with one another, and the blood of Jesus his Son cleanses us from all sin. If we say that we have no sin, we deceive ourselves, and the truth is not in us. If we confess our sins, he who is faithful and just will forgive us our sins and cleanse us from all unrighteousness. If we say that we have not sinned, we make him a liar, and his word is not in us.

My little children, I am writing these things to you so that you may not sin. But if anyone does sin, we have an advocate with the Father, Jesus Christ the righteous; and he is the atoning sacrifice for our sins, and not for ours only but also for the sins of the whole world.

1 JOHN 1:5—2:2

In contrast to the ways in which we trip ourselves up in the spiritual life, sin is a real and pressing problem. Although the *Cloud* author lived at a time when the church's discipline of confession to a priest and penance undertaken for those sins was a normal part of the Christian life, he does not teach that we can overcome sin and its effects by ourselves. 'Fast as much as you like, watch far into the night, rise long before dawn, discipline your body... and you would still gain nothing. The desire and tendency toward sin would remain in your heart.'[18]

It is right to use what the church provides as a way of clearing the decks before beginning the work of contemplation, but it is that work itself which 'dries up the root and ground of the sin that is always there, even after one's confession and however busy one is in holy things'.[19] Even so, the author knows that it is not always this simple; an awareness of sin remains, and we know ourselves to be always falling away from God. What do we do then? We should not analyse our sense of sin, says the *Cloud* author. 'Let yourself experience sin as a *lump*, realizing that it is yourself, but without defining it precisely.'[20] Do not think too much of what you are—simply that you are. But simply staying there, with a sense of being a sinful person, would be too much to bear, so he goes on to suggest a remedy.

Take good, gracious God just as he is, and without further ado lay him on your sick self just as you are, for all the world as if he were a poultice! Or to put it in other words, lift up your sick self just as you are, and through your longing strive to touch good, gracious God just as he is... Don't give a thought, however ingenious, to any or all of your own qualities, or God's, whether those attributes are pure or wretched, grace-given or natural, divine or human. All that matters now is that this unseeing awareness of your basic self should be carried up with glad, vigorous love and, by the grace of the Holy Spirit, united with the precious being of God, just as he in himself, no more and no less.[21]

We can see how the author applies the principles of contemplative prayer that he is teaching to this particular question of the sense of sin. Just as we are to leave behind all thoughts of God in our prayer, so we are to leave behind all thoughts of our own unworthiness, beyond the global sense that we cannot save ourselves, and that sin is like a lump within us. We are to be clear-eyed about ourselves, but not despairing, knowing that God as he is can encompass all that is wrong with us as we are.

Then, if thoughts of our past sin or new temptations arise during prayer, we should 'bravely step beyond them'.[22] The author suggests a couple of 'dodges' to use when this seems impossibly difficult.

The first is to ignore these thoughts or temptations. 'Do everything you can to act as if you did not know that they were so strongly pushing in between you and God. Try to look, as it were, over their shoulders, seeking something else—which is God.'[23] If even this does not work, then he makes the startling suggestion that we should simply surrender, acknowledge powerlessness, and stop fighting: 'For in doing this you commend yourself to God in the midst of your enemies and admit the radical impotence of your nature.'[24]

PRAYER

God of sinners, give me the honesty to confess my sins, to acknowledge my sinfulness; and the humility to turn to you, knowing that only you can heal. Let me come to you as I am, and know you as you are, my healer and redeemer. Amen.

Thursday

LONGING LOVE

Beloved, let us love one another, because love is from God; everyone who loves is born of God and knows God. Whoever does not love does not know God, for God is love. God's love was revealed among us in this way: God sent his only Son into the world so that we might live through him. In this is love, not that we loved God but that he loved us and sent his Son to be the atoning sacrifice for our sins. Beloved, since God loved us so much, we also ought to love one another. No one has ever seen God; if we love one another, God lives in us, and his love is perfected in us.

By this we know that we abide in him and he in us, because he has given us of his Spirit. And we have seen and do testify that the Father has sent his Son as the Saviour of the world. God abides in those who confess that Jesus is the Son of God, and they abide in God. So we have known and believe the love that God has for us.

God is love, and those who abide in love abide in God, and God abides in them. Love has been perfected among us in this: that we may have boldness on the day of judgment, because as he is, so are we in this world.

1 JOHN 4:7–17

We ended yesterday in quite a dark place, overcome by temptation and throwing ourselves on the mercy of God, but it would be wrong to allow sin and sorrow to have the last words. The *Cloud* author, while taking sin seriously, sees love as far more important. Quoting the story in Luke's Gospel of the woman who came to Jesus in the house of Simon the Pharisee and washed Jesus' feet (Luke 7:36–50), which we will read tomorrow, he reminds his readers that she is forgiven because she loved much: 'Not for her great sorrow; not for her anxiety over her sins; not for her humility as she contemplated her wretchedness; but, surely, because she loved much.'[25]

Very early in *The Cloud of Unknowing*, the author addresses his disciple: 'Your whole life now must be one of longing, if you are to achieve perfection. And this longing must be in the depths of your will, put there by God, with your consent.'[26] Love and longing are the strongest connections between God and humanity because 'God is love, and those who abide in love abide in God, and God abides in them'.

Always God takes the initiative in this love. 'And so, with exquisite kindness, he awakened desire within you, and binding it fast with the leash of love's longing, drew you closer to himself,'[27] the author writes to his disciple. This 'longing love' is very characteristic of the *Cloud* author and other writers of his period. In contrast to the joy of being in the presence of the beloved, *desiderium*, or longing love, was love in the absence of the beloved. We can see how well it fits with the way of prayer he is teaching. The contemplative must be willing to be in a state of 'unknowing', and to let go of any desire for the things of God, for a sense of God's presence, for the consolations he offers, in order to know him as he really is.

It is our love and our desire, answering God's love of us and desire for us, that will bring us to know God. In this life we cannot see God as he is, so our love will always be in the absence of the beloved, never entirely fulfilled. The cloud will always be between us, and only love can penetrate it.

Of course, it is impossible in this life to see and possess God fully but, with his grace and in his own time, it is possible to taste something of him as he is in himself. And so with great longing for him enter into this cloud. Or rather, I should say, let God awaken your longing and draw you to himself in this cloud while you strive with the help of his grace to forget everything else.[28]

The author can use language of great determination: 'Beat away at this cloud of unknowing between you and God with that sharp dart of longing love.'[29] This is no prescription for total passivity, waiting for God to do it all for us. Instead, there is a paradoxical recognition that while we cannot, by our goodness or determination, break through to God, yet by our intention to know him we make ourselves available and attentive so that we recognize the moments when he makes himself known. The *Cloud* author describes these moments as like a spark from a fire, springing up suddenly and as quickly gone.

Brief though they are, however, like any experience of love, they can change everything, making the struggle worthwhile and causing our own love to flare up into new life.

PRAYER

God of love, fashion my love for you into a sharp dart of longing, and let my desire for you be penetrating and persevering. Kindle the flame of love within me now, and keep alive in me the knowledge that one day I will see you face to face, and love you for ever. Amen.

Friday

FORGETFUL OF SELF

One of the Pharisees asked Jesus to eat with him, and he went into the Pharisee's house and took his place at the table. And a woman in the city, who was a sinner, having learned that he was eating in the Pharisee's house, brought an alabaster jar of ointment. She stood behind him at his feet, weeping, and began to bathe his feet with her tears and to dry them with her hair. Then she continued kissing his feet and anointing them with the ointment. Now when the Pharisee who had invited him saw it, he said to himself, 'If this man were a prophet, he would have known who and what kind of woman this is who is touching him—that she is a sinner.' Jesus spoke up and said to him, 'Simon, I have something to say to you.' 'Teacher,' he replied, 'speak.' 'A certain creditor had two debtors; one owed five hundred denarii, and the other fifty. When they could not pay, he cancelled the debts for both of them. Now which of them will love him more?' Simon answered, 'I suppose the one for whom he cancelled the greater debt.' And Jesus said to him, 'You have judged rightly.' Then turning towards the woman, he said to Simon, 'Do you see this woman? I entered your house; you gave me no water for my feet, but she has bathed my feet with her tears and dried them with her hair. You gave me no kiss, but from the time I came in she has not stopped kissing my feet. You did not anoint my head with oil, but she has anointed my feet with ointment. Therefore, I tell you, her sins, which were many, have been forgiven; hence she has shown great love. But the one to whom little is forgiven, loves little.' Then he said to her, 'Your sins

are forgiven.' But those who were at the table with him began to say among themselves, 'Who is this who even forgives sins?' And he said to the woman, 'Your faith has saved you; go in peace.'
LUKE 7:36–50

Traditionally, the woman in this story is seen as Mary Magdalene. As we saw last week, many medieval writers blended together Mary Magdalene with Mary of Bethany and the sinful woman of this story, to create one composite 'Mary', a sinner whose great love for Jesus brought her forgiveness and healing, and who was also called to contemplation.

Although biblical scholars today would treat each story separately, there is a richness in the medieval approach too, and today I want to use their way to look at two themes that are important to the *Cloud* author. We saw yesterday how he wrote of this woman as one who was forgiven because of her love for Jesus. In the story, Jesus does not deny that she is a sinner, and the *Cloud* author, who also takes sin seriously, surprisingly writes that 'it often happens that some who have been hardened, habitual sinners arrive at the perfection of this work sooner than those who have never sinned grievously. God is truly wonderful in lavishing his grace on anyone he chooses.'[30]

Perhaps it is the same passion that led them to sin which, when turned to repentance and love of God, moves them on more quickly in the life of the spirit? As we have seen, the *Cloud* author counsels not dwelling on past sin or analysing it in detail, and this turning away from self towards God is a general principle for him.

The woman in this story seems to have been entirely forgetful of self, in a way that many of the onlookers no doubt found embarrassing. She was completely focused on Jesus, and unaware of the effect of her actions on others. The *Cloud* author commends this: 'So whenever you look at what it is you are doing, and realize that it is yourself you are conscious of and not God, seek to be sincerely sorry, and long to be aware of God.'[31] He then goes on to a poignant image: 'For now you are your own cross… This is where you see your need to feel sorrow, and your desire to be rid of self-awareness.'[32]

As a modern writer puts it, 'Preoccupation with self remains the pain of the human condition',[33] and in the end it doesn't really matter whether this is preoccupation with our own sin and sorrow or with our successes and goodness. In an image worthy of the *Cloud* author himself, another modern writer comments, 'Sorrow would harden the obsessive content of past misdeeds, while naked longing unfastened the will to receive greater forgiveness.'[34]

This longing, and a willingness to express it, is a mark of all three 'Marys'. It is perhaps most striking in today's story, but it is also present in the story of Mary of Bethany sitting at the feet of Jesus to hear his teaching, careless of her sister's irritation at being left with all the work, and in Mary Magdalene's unrestrained weeping outside the tomb of Jesus, longing at least to see his beloved body one last time.

Whether we see them as three separate women or as the one penitent contemplative of the *Cloud* author, they have much to teach us through their unselfconscious self-giving to God.

PRAYER

Take from me, gracious God, all that separates me from you—my sense of past sin, my pride in present achievements, my anxieties for the future. Make me self-forgetful as I gaze on you, and let me know the joy of finding my true self in you. Amen.

Saturday

WAITING IN THE DARKNESS

Now Moses used to take the tent and pitch it outside the camp, far off from the camp; he called it the tent of meeting. And everyone who sought the Lord would go out to the tent of meeting, which was outside the camp. Whenever Moses went out to the tent, all the people would rise and stand, each of them, at the entrance of their tents and watch Moses until he had gone into the tent. When Moses entered the tent, the pillar of cloud would descend and stand at the entrance of the tent, and the Lord would speak with Moses... Thus the Lord used to speak to Moses face to face, as one speaks to a friend...

Moses said to the Lord, 'See, you have said to me, "Bring up this people"; but you have not let me know whom you will send with me. Yet you have said, "I know you by name, and you have also found favour in my sight." Now if I have found favour in your sight, show me your ways, so that I may know you and find favour in your sight...'

The Lord said to Moses, 'I will do the very thing that you have asked; for you have found favour in my sight, and I know you by name.' Moses said, 'Show me your glory, I pray.' And he said, 'I will make all my goodness pass before you, and will proclaim before you the name "The Lord"; and I will be gracious to whom I will be gracious, and will show mercy on whom I will show mercy. But,' he said, 'you cannot see my face; for no one shall see me and live.' And the Lord continued, 'See, there is a place by me where you shall stand on the rock; and while my glory passes by

I will put you in a cleft of the rock, and I will cover you with my hand until I have passed by; then I will take away my hand, and you shall see my back; but my face shall not be seen.'
EXODUS 33:7–23 (ABRIDGED)

For many medieval and earlier writers, Moses is a great example of the human journey towards God. Dionysius, in his *Mystical Theology*, which the *Cloud* author translated, uses the account of Moses' ascent of Mount Sinai to describe three traditional stages of the journey. First, Moses must be purified, corresponding to repentance and forgiveness of sin; then he makes the arduous journey to the mountain top, but still he does not see God himself, only 'the place where God was'.[35] Finally, Moses goes on alone into 'the thick darkness where God was' (Exodus 20:21b).

Then Dionysius goes on, in a passage rich in paradox:

Into this supreme and dazzling darkness we pray that we may come, that by not seeing and not knowing we may see and know him who is beyond all seeing and knowing through this very act of not seeing or knowing; and at this supreme peak of being, by dismissing all things that are, that we may praise him who is himself above all.[36]

Dionysius, and the *Cloud* author with him, acknowledge that this may seem beyond reason:

For when we are considering matters to do with the Most High the very words on which we base such consideration actually limit our understanding. So here in this present book, when we are entering the darkness that is beyond mind, not only do we find that words are inadequate, but everything we say seems fantastic and utterly irrational.[37]

This is a classical description of one of the two traditional ways of mystical prayer in the Christian tradition, and reflects the apophatic tradition, which is 'negative, devoid of images, reflecting God's essential unknowability to the human intellect'. The other way is the cataphatic: 'positive and image-filled, reflecting the revelatory nature of all created things as they witness to their Creator'.[38]

The *Cloud* author stands firmly in the apophatic tradition: 'learn to be at home in this darkness,'[39] he counsels his disciple at the start of his book, and nearly all his writings are an expansion of this simple instruction, explaining how it can be done, dealing with the difficulties that inevitably arise, and encouraging the disciple to persevere with this difficult but rewarding path. Only in this way, he believes, will the disciple come to share Moses' experience, itself paradoxical, of speaking to God face to face, yet being able to see only his back.

The unknowable God wills to make himself known, but as and how he wills, and not by our techniques, goodness, or determination. Our longing and our love make us ready to receive him, and our commitment to contemplative prayer, when we are called to it, provides the seedbed for our knowledge of God to grow and flourish. In this process the author of *The Cloud* is a guide to us, as much as he was to his unknown disciple so many centuries ago.

PRAYER

Today there are no words. Simply sit in silence and turn all your longing towards God.

PRAYING WITH 'THE CLOUD OF UNKNOWING'

It would be very strange to spend a week with the author of a book that is all about prayer, and not try to pray in the way which he teaches. All the information needed is there in *The Cloud of Unknowing*, but it isn't always very systematic. A more straightforward way in to this type of prayer is probably through the practice of Centring Prayer, which is founded on the teaching of *The Cloud*. It was begun by Fr William Meninger and developed by Fr Thomas Keating, both American Benedictine monks. Another monk, Fr M. Basil Pennington, has also written on this way of prayer. You will find details of books and a website at the end of the book.

The simple guidelines that Thomas Keating has produced are the basis of what I am suggesting here.

1. Choose a sacred word of one, or at most two, syllables. Examples are God, Jesus, Abba, Amen, Love, Mercy, Stillness, Faith, Yes. The word is a symbol of our intention to consent to God's presence and action within us during the time of prayer. Having chosen the word, do not change it during the time of prayer.
2. Sit comfortably, with your back straight and your eyes closed. Use your sacred word, silently, as a symbol of your consent to God's presence and action within you. Do not aim to recite the word constantly, but allow it to fall away if this happens naturally.
3. When you notice that you are engaged with thoughts, return very gently to the sacred word. 'Thoughts' is a broad term including feelings, memories, plans, commentary and spiritual experiences.

4. Continue for about 20 minutes. At the end of the period, remain in silence with your eyes closed for a couple of minutes.

You might like to commit yourself to a 20-minute period of this kind of prayer each day this week. If you are part of a group, share your experience with each other.

WORKING WITH A SPIRITUAL FRIEND

The author of *The Cloud* wrote to his 'friend in God'. Although we do not have the other side of the correspondence, it seems that these two men corresponded and perhaps met to teach and learn about the spiritual life. This kind of relationship has always been part of the Christian life, from the days of the fourth-century desert fathers, the early Egyptian monks, until now. Those who are further along the path have offered help to those starting off, and those starting off have sought out someone to advise them.

Have you experienced this kind of spiritual relationship? If so, reflect on how you use it. Are there areas of your life that are out of bounds? Are there problems that you do not bring to your friend, or difficulties that you do not acknowledge? Give thanks for this gift of God in your life, and for what it has given you over the years.

If you haven't experienced it, might it be useful to find someone to fulfil this role? We all, at times, find ourselves stuck in our spiritual lives, and sharing this experience with someone else can help to bring a fresh perspective and perhaps ways of moving forward. At the very least, it can provide encouragement to stick with what may be difficult.

Your own church would be the natural place to begin your search for a spiritual friend or guide; there may be someone you already know who could fulfil this role for you. If you would prefer someone you don't already know, your church should be able to suggest ways of finding someone in your area.

REPENTING

Lent is, of course, a traditional time to acknowledge and repent of both our specific sins and our sinfulness as an attitude. If there is anything particular that is weighing you down and holding you back on your journey, you may like to make this Lenten period a time to deal with it. In your own prayer, look honestly at what is coming between you and God, acknowledge it to God, and then let it go, believing that 'If we confess our sins, he who is faithful and just will forgive us our sins and cleanse us from all unrighteousness' (1 John 1:9). Follow the advice of this week's author and lay God on your sick self as a poultice; don't wait until you feel you are worthy of God's love, but come 'just as you are, and through your longing strive to touch good, gracious God just as he is'.

If it is part of your tradition to confess sin privately to a priest or to another person, you may like to do that too. If it is not part of your tradition, might you consider it anyway? While God can and does forgive whatever we confess directly to him, it can be immensely reassuring and strengthening to hear the words of forgiveness addressed to us by another person, speaking in the name of God.

John and Charles Wesley

Sunday

JUSTIFIED BY FAITH

For this reason it depends on faith, in order that the promise may rest on grace and be guaranteed to all his descendants, not only to the adherents of the law but also to those who share the faith of Abraham... Hoping against hope, he believed that he would become 'the father of many nations', according to what was said, 'So numerous shall your descendants be.' He did not weaken in faith when he considered his own body, which was already as good as dead (for he was about a hundred years old), or when he considered the barrenness of Sarah's womb. No distrust made him waver concerning the promise of God, but he grew strong in his faith as he gave glory to God, being fully convinced that God was able to do what he had promised. Therefore his faith 'was reckoned to him as righteousness'.

ROMANS 4:16, 18–22

The apostle Paul has a lot to answer for. He was a wonderful theologian (though not always easy to understand), and a great example of missionary zeal, but his conversion experience has often become an unhelpful model of how conversion happens. His dramatic experience on the way to Damascus (you can read the story in Acts 9, and Paul's own account of what happened in Acts 22) can make other conversions seem pale and unconvincing. His was a complete turnaround, from persecuting Christians to becoming one himself, through an unmistakable experience of God and a voice that told him clearly what to do next.

For most Christians through the ages, conversion has been a less dramatic event. Coming to faith, learning to rest on God's grace and to hope in his promises, is a slower process for most of us than it was for Paul, perhaps proceeding in fits and starts, with two steps forward and one back over a considerable period. Although, for some, there is a definitive moment in this process at which they can point and say, 'That was the moment when I became a Christian', for others there may be a number of converting events and moments, each of which takes the journey a stage further.

John and Charles Wesley, the founders of Methodism, are our companions for this week. Each had a moment that they saw as crucial, but they experienced it as part of a much longer process of seeking and struggling.

John and Charles Wesley were part of a very large vicarage family, at Epworth in Lincolnshire. John was born in 1703, the 16th child of Samuel and Susanna Wesley, and Charles four years later. It was a Puritan household, with the Bible at the heart of its life, and John later described himself as a man of one book—the Bible. Both brothers studied at Christ Church, Oxford; John was ordained deacon in 1725 and priest in 1728, by which time he was a fellow of Lincoln College. In 1728 Charles had a 'spiritual awakening' but it was a further ten years before each of the brothers had their defining conversion experience and received the inner assurance of faith for which they longed.

In the meantime, they studied the Christian classics and gathered around them a group of fellow students, nicknamed the Holy Club, who studied the Bible together and were committed to a systematic and disciplined life of prayer and regular communion. They also studied together the writings of the Fathers of the church, looking back to the early centuries of the church's life for guidance. Their study and prayer were balanced by involvement with those in need. John visited prisoners and the sick, helped to start a school, and discovered that he could live on £28 a year.

In September 1735, Samuel Wesley died, and John and Charles, together with two others from the Holy Club, travelled to Georgia as missionaries to the Indians and colonists, arriving in February 1736. It was a leap into the unknown, and one that proved very difficult for both brothers (the records of the colony speak bluntly of John 'run away 3 Dec 1737'), but it did provoke a re-examination of their spiritual lives. When they returned to London early in 1738, they had changed already and were seeking further change. In fact, some churches refused to allow John to preach to them on his return; his search for an experience of God's assurance, for 'justifying, saving faith, a full reliance on the blood of Christ shed for *me*, a trust in him, as *my* Christ',[1] was taking him away from the conventional faith of his day.

Finally, on 24 May 1738, at a meeting at Aldersgate Street, John received the assurance he sought. The speaker was reading Luther's Preface to the Epistle to the Romans:

About a quarter before nine, while he was describing the change which God works in the heart through faith in Christ, I felt my heart strangely warmed. I felt I did trust in Christ, Christ alone for salvation; and an assurance was given me that he had taken away my sins, even mine, and saved me from the law of sin and death.[2]

Charles had had a similar experience three days earlier. God's grace had found both John and Charles Wesley, and their lives would go on being changed by it.

PRAYER

God of grace, give me always the assurance of your grace and the faith that brings life. Make me willing to receive these gifts in your time and in your way. Amen.

Monday

THE GIFT OF GRACE

But now, apart from law, the righteousness of God has been disclosed, and is attested by the law and the prophets, the righteousness of God through faith in Jesus Christ for all who believe. For there is no distinction, since all have sinned and fall short of the glory of God; they are now justified by his grace as a gift, through the redemption that is in Christ Jesus, whom God put forward as a sacrifice of atonement by his blood, effective through faith. He did this to show his righteousness, because in his divine forbearance he had passed over the sins previously committed; it was to prove at the present time that he himself is righteous and that he justifies the one who has faith in Jesus.

ROMANS 3:21–26

As Paul's upbringing as a devout Jew affected how he experienced and described his new life as a Christian, so were John and Charles Wesley's theology and practice affected by their upbringing at Epworth and experiences of faith as adults. Their mother Susanna was 'a woman of very strong character who ruled the children through a benevolent despotism that involved "breaking their wills" by the time they were aged one'.[3] Life was frugal and very disciplined. After John barely survived a fire at the Rectory when he was seven, Susanna, feeling that he had been spared for a purpose, made particular efforts to encourage his spiritual development, and spent time with him every week, teaching and advising.

During their difficult time in Georgia, both brothers came under the influence of the Moravians, a German group who emphasized inner assurance and justification by faith alone. In London, another Moravian, Peter Böhler, guided John as he sought inner peace in a bewildering time. After the experience at Aldersgate Street, John travelled to Germany to visit the Moravian leader, Zinzendorf. Back in London, he belonged for a time to a Moravian group, the Fetter Lane Society, but came to believe that their total emphasis on justification by faith ran the risk of neglecting the need to respond to God's grace, especially through the sacraments, and to engage in good works. In the end he separated himself from them.

The Moravian stress on faith alone had probably been, for both brothers, a necessary corrective to the emphasis in their upbringing on wrath, punishment and working for one's salvation. It helped them to move towards a faith that saw Jesus as a friend, and to a better balance between law and grace in their lives.

The Wesleys trod a difficult and narrow path in their teaching on the relationship between law and grace. Keeping the sense of grace as pure gift, a work of God through Jesus Christ, while also asserting the need to respond to and work with this grace, requires a subtle holding together of what can seem contradictory ideas, an ability to live with 'both/and' rather than 'either/or'. Perhaps John Wesley gives as good a description as any of this strange state in his journal entry for the day of his conversion at Aldersgate.

After my return home, I was much buffeted with temptations, but cried out and they fled away. They returned again and again. I as often lifted up my eyes and he sent me help from his holy place. And herein I found [in what] the difference between this and my former state chiefly consisted. I was striving, yea, fighting with all my might under the law, as well as under grace. But then I was sometimes, if not often, conquered; now, I was always conqueror. [4]

The struggle and the need to work had not gone away, but an assurance of victory through Christ's work had been given.

For both brothers, the Eucharist was central as one of the signs of God's free grace, and they taught and practised frequent Holy Communion at a time when it was rare. In fact, Church of England bishops of the time were encouraging their clergy to provide only one service of Communion between Pentecost (early summer) and Christmas, while the early Methodists were expected to be at Communion every Sunday. It was one of the ways by which they became and remained united with Christ, able to draw on his grace for their daily lives. John used the biblical image of the branch and the vine: 'For our perfection is not like that of a tree, which flourishes by the sap derived from its own root, but… like that of a branch, which united to the vine, bears fruit; but severed from it, *is dried up and withered*.'[5]

In his hymn 'Author of life divine', Charles wrote of the way in which our souls are nourished and sustained in the eucharist with 'fresh supplies of love'.[6] The God who saved through Christ's work on the cross did not expect his people to live solely on the memory of that act, but continued to pour out his grace to all those who chose to remain 'united to the vine'.

PRAYER

Righteous God, keep me at rest in your love and your redemption, and active in my response to you and my work in your service. Amen.

Tuesday

FAITH, WORKS AND LOVE

Therefore just as one man's trespass led to condemnation for all, so one man's act of righteousness leads to justification and life for all. For just as by the one man's disobedience the many were made sinners, so by the one man's obedience the many will be made righteous. But law came in, with the result that the trespass multiplied; but where sin increased, grace abounded all the more, so that, just as sin exercised dominion in death, so grace might also exercise dominion through justification leading to eternal life through Jesus Christ our Lord.

ROMANS 5:18–21

For me, one of the pleasures of taking up a new activity or becoming interested in a new area of knowledge is learning the new vocabulary that goes with it. At its worst, of course, it can become jargon, a language that the initiated use to keep the uninitiated out. At best, though, new words open up new ideas and different ways of thinking.

Paul's theological language, the words he uses and the way in which he uses them, have been studied minutely over the generations, especially some of the passages from Romans on sin, justification and grace. People have come to very different conclusions as a result of their study.

Some of these conclusions are relevant to our journey with the Wesleys, because they clearly took one side of a continuing debate, between Calvinism and Arminianism. Calvinism was formulated by John Calvin, the 16th-century Swiss pastor. Among the key elements of his theology are that scripture is the only rule of faith, that since the fall of Adam humans have no free will, that we are justified by faith alone, without works, and that only those who have been predestined by God for salvation can be saved. Arminianism stems from the work of Jacobus Arminius, a Dutch theologian, born in 1560. He reacted in particular against the doctrine of predestination, and insisted that God's sovereignty and human free will could co-exist and that Jesus died for all people and not only the elect.

John Wesley wrestled with the issues on which these two groups disagreed as he sought the assurance he longed for. In his journal entry for January 1738, he recalls how he had been warned against an overemphasis on works or on faith alone, and believes that he had kept a balanced view, 'having from the beginning valued both faith and the means of grace and good works, not on their own account, but as believing that God, who had appointed them, would by them bring me in due time to the mind that was in Christ'. But then, he recalls, 'I fell among some Lutheran and Calvinist authors, whose confused and indigested accounts magnified faith to such an amazing size that it quite hid all the rest of the comandments.' He recognizes that their overemphasis was a reaction to Catholic theology, which seemed to exalt merit and good works above everything else, so that 'they plunged at once into the other extreme'. He concludes in words that many of us will echo in the face of theological controversies: 'In this labyrinth I was utterly lost.'[7]

He did not remain lost, however; through his experiences with the Moravians, the conversion at Aldersgate and his continued study, he came to hold the Arminian view, and it greatly influenced both his preaching and the hymns that Charles wrote. There were other groups of Methodists who took the Calvinist position.

'Where sin increased, grace abounded all the more': these words of Paul have been interpreted in an unhelpful way—antinomianism. This is the conviction that we should continue in sin so that grace may abound, and the Wesleys firmly rejected this position. A substantial section of the definitive Methodist hymn book of 1780 was given to penitence, and many of the hymns spoke of the struggle to find release through God's Spirit from the grip of sin and self-centredness. This sense of struggle is brilliantly captured in the hymn 'Come, O thou traveller unknown', in which Charles interweaves the story of Jacob struggling with God at Peniel (Genesis 32:24–32) with the Christian's response to God's Holy Spirit. It ends triumphantly with the line 'Thy nature and thy name is Love'.[8]

This was the controlling theme of the Wesleys' theology. Where the Calvinists took to its logical conclusion their belief in the omnipotence of God, which ended by leaving no room for human initiative or free will, John and Charles put love at the centre, love that wanted all people to be saved and was available to all. But, as we saw yesterday when we looked at grace, it was a love that required a response: 'God's grace, though boundless, is not cheap; he requires holiness as well as faith. But the perfect love that he requires of us stems from the fact that the ground of his being is love, and that love is available to all, whether beggar or prostitute, worthy or not.'[9]

'For all, for all, my Saviour died,' Charles wrote, and a modern author comments, 'Both the "my" and the "all" were of paramount importance.'[10] God's love was freely available to all, but each individual had to make their personal response of love to what God had done in Christ for each of them.

PRAYER

God of all people, thank you for your desire that all people should know and love you. Help me to live today in a way that shows your love to everyone. Amen.

Wednesday

PREACHING SALVATION

You were dead through the trespasses and sins in which you once lived, following the course of this world, following the ruler of the power of the air, the spirit that is now at work among those who are disobedient. All of us once lived among them in the passions of our flesh, following the desires of flesh and senses, and we were by nature children of wrath, like everyone else. But God, who is rich in mercy, out of the great love with which he loved us even when we were dead through our trespasses, made us alive together with Christ—by grace you have been saved—and raised us up with him and seated us with him in the heavenly places in Christ Jesus, so that in the ages to come he might show the immeasurable riches of his grace in kindness toward us in Christ Jesus. For by grace you have been saved through faith, and this is not your own doing; it is the gift of God—not the result of works, so that no one may boast. For we are what he has made us, created in Christ Jesus for good works, which God prepared beforehand to be our way of life.

EPHESIANS 2:1–10

If God offered his grace and love to all people, there was a great impetus to evangelism, to make sure that as many people as possible heard the message of the gospel and had an opportunity to make their response. After 1738, John Wesley therefore spent much of his life preaching.

It was on 2 April 1739, in Bristol, that he preached the first of the open-air sermons that were to be a major feature of the rest of his life. He had been asked to deputize for George Whitefield, the later leader of the Calvinistic Methodists, while Whitefield visited America. John went in fear and trembling, but the sermon, on the text 'The Spirit of the Lord is upon me...', was successful, and a crowd of three thousand people heard it. It was a turning point in his life, as he moved from learning from others to teaching others. In his preaching, the hymns of Charles played a key role, preparing the people for John's sermons and reinforcing his teaching. For the rest of John's life, he travelled tirelessly throughout the British Isles, 225,000 miles in all, often on horseback, and preached 40,000 sermons.

In this work, he was not necessarily following his natural inclinations. In his journal for 1759, twenty years into his ministry, he recorded:

On Monday and Tuesday evening I preached abroad, near the Keelmen's Hospital, to twice the people we should have had at the house. What marvel the devil does not love field-preaching? Neither do I: I love a commodious room, a soft cushion, an handsome pulpit. But where is my zeal, if I do not trample all these under foot, in order to save one more soul?[11]

This work could be dangerous. Crowds gathered and were sometimes violent. Once, when preaching in the Potteries in Staffordshire, the noise was so loud that John could not be heard. He attempted to go into a house whose door stood open, but one of the mob grabbed him by the hair and hauled him back into the crowd, who swept him the whole length of the main street. As they went, John continued to speak to those near him. Gradually he won over some, who became his protectors against the mob, until finally 'a little before ten, God brought me safe to Wednesbury; having lost only one flap of my waistcoat, and a little skin from one of my hands'.[12]

Conversion to a genuine and personal faith in Christ was the purpose of many of Wesley's sermons, but that was not the end. If his hearers had been made 'alive together with Christ', raised with him and brought to heaven with him, this had consequences for how they were to live the rest of their lives. On the morning of 24 May 1738, John had read the opening of the second letter of Peter: 'His divine power has given us everything needed for life and godliness, through the knowledge of him who called us by his own glory and goodness. Thus he has given us, through these things, his precious and very great promises, so that through them you may escape from the corruption that is in the world because of lust, and may become participants in the divine nature' (2 Peter 1:3–4).

Godliness, holiness, becoming participants in the divine nature, were to be the lifelong programme for those converted by John's preaching and the singing of Charles' hymns. It sounds daunting, and it is, but it is not impossible. John knew that his converts would go wrong again, but they would still be guided by perfect love, the love that God gives through our co-operation with his loving purposes. 'The test was always fidelity to the mind of Christ, love of enemies, a heart purged of "self and pride", malice and all un-charitableness.'[13]

PRAYER

Holy God, kindle in my heart the desire to speak of you, and the willingness to go beyond my comfort zones in doing so. By your love, transform me day by day into your likeness. Amen.

Thursday

THE HARVEST OF RIGHTEOUSNESS

I thank my God every time I remember you, constantly praying with joy in every one of my prayers for all of you, because of your sharing in the gospel from the first day until now. I am confident of this, that the one who began a good work among you will bring it to completion by the day of Jesus Christ... And this is my prayer, that your love may overflow more and more with knowledge and full insight to help you to determine what is best, so that on the day of Christ you may be pure and blameless, having produced the harvest of righteousness that comes through Jesus Christ for the glory and praise of God.

PHILIPPIANS 1:3–6, 9–11

'A good work' was begun in many people through John Wesley's preaching and Charles' hymns, but how was it to be continued and brought to completion? It was the brothers' answer to this question, gradually worked out over many years, that led to their followers' being given the name 'Methodists'. It was not their aim to start a new church: both brothers remained Anglicans until the end of their lives, and argued against those who wanted to separate themselves from a church that they saw as lukewarm and ineffective. John expected the early Methodists to go to their parish church for Holy Communion, but also provided other opportunities for teaching, learning and mutual support. It was these societies, bands and classes, a 'method' for deepening the spirituality of those who had come to a new faith and enabling them to pass their faith on, that led to others naming them Methodists.

In this, the brothers responded to the needs of those they served. They did not begin by drawing up a plan and then fitting people into it. One writer describes what they did as 'prayerful improvisation' and John himself, looking back in 1787, recalled that he and his brother had had no plan.

They only went hither and thither, wherever they had a prospect of saving souls. But when more and more asked, 'What must I do to be saved?' they were desired to meet all together. Twelve came the first Thursday night; forty the next, soon after, a hundred. And they continued to increase till, three or four and twenty years ago, the London Society amounted to about 2,800.[14]

Societies were formed wherever John went to preach. As they became too big to function as one group, they divided into bands, or classes. Each class, which had a maximum of twelve members, met weekly on a Thursday for fellowship. This system did not appear in a vacuum; John applied what he had learned in his family (touchingly, Thursday had been the day on which his mother met with John as a child to attend to his spiritual life and growth), in the Holy Club at Oxford, in Georgia, and with the Moravians. All of these groups had had elements of mutual support and accountability, but it was John's genius to create an entire and interconnected system out of his earlier experiences.

Each Methodist belonged to a class, classes were joined in societies, societies were joined in circuits, and the circuits joined together in an annual conference, superintended by John and Charles Wesley themselves. The class was no soft option. The only qualification for membership was a desire for holiness, and the work of the class consisted of opening worship, followed by each member of the group in turn giving an account of the state of their soul and confessing their sins and temptations. Others in the group could comment on the confession, and give guidance. It was a group form of spiritual direction.

John drew up questions to be asked, rules to be kept, and

schemes of self-examination to be used, which show the seriousness of the undertaking. For example, one of the questions to be asked of those wishing to join a class was: 'Is it your desire and design to be on this, and all other occasions, entirely open, so as to speak everything that is in your heart without exceptions, without disguise, and without reserve?'[15] A daunting undertaking! Every part of life was to be ruled by God, and this involved weekly Communion and daily prayer and reading of scripture, almsgiving, honesty in buying and selling, abstinence from alcohol, and 'to wear no needless ornaments, such as rings, earrings, necklaces, lace, ruffles'.[16]

With so many rules and such intense self-examination, there was a real risk of hopelessness and gloom descending. But John, in one of his letters, said that this need not be so: 'There is no manner of necessity that this self-knowledge should make us miserable. Certainly the highest degree of it is well consistent both with peace and joy in the Holy Ghost.'[17]

The 'prayerful improvisation' of the Wesleys helped to bring into being what Paul in his letter to the Philippians prayed for: mature Christians, overflowing with knowledge and insight, and producing the harvest of righteousness.

PRAYER

God of community, thank you for my fellow Christians, for all who build me up and hold me accountable. Make me humble and open in my fellowship, and keep me faithful to the work you are doing in me. Amen.

Friday

THEOLOGY WITH WINGS

Be careful then how you live, not as unwise people but as wise, making the most of the time, because the days are evil. So do not be foolish, but understand what the will of the Lord is. Do not get drunk with wine, for that is debauchery; but be filled with the Spirit, as you sing psalms and hymns and spiritual songs among yourselves, singing and making melody to the Lord in your hearts, giving thanks to God the Father at all times and for everything in the name of our Lord Jesus Christ.

EPHESIANS 5:15–20

'He bids us build each other up'[18] runs a line in one of Charles Wesley's many hymns, and this, speaking so precisely to the Methodist system of societies and classes, is an excellent example of the way in which Charles' hymns dovetailed with and supported John's work of preaching and organization.

So far, John has been our main companion this week. He was the one who wrote journals, letters and books, whose sermons we have, and who wrote down the rules for the emerging Methodist movement. But now Charles takes centre stage as we look at the place of music and singing. We take for granted nowadays that most acts of worship will include singing, but this was not the case for the Wesleys. In fact, until 1819, a Church of England incumbent could be taken to court for allowing hymns to be sung in his church.

Like John, Charles studied at Christ Church, Oxford, where he became a lecturer. It was Charles who founded the Holy Club, although John took over its leadership when he returned to Oxford in 1729, after ordination. Both brothers went to Georgia, but Charles returned before John, in July 1736. Like his brother, Charles entered an intense period of seeking, and, three days before John, received the inward assurance of faith that he sought. He had already written hymns before this experience, but now they changed, becoming more immediate, more personal, and more convinced that the grace of God that he had found for himself was available to all people. During the rest of his life, until his death in 1788, Charles wrote nearly 5000 hymns, often setting them to popular tunes of the day. Unlike John, Charles had a happy marriage, and although he did preach widely, his life was more settled as the spiritual leader of the Methodists in Bristol and later in London.

Charles' hymns were expressions of personal faith, but they were also doctrinally sound, built on his wide reading. Ideas can be found in them that stem from the church fathers, from Thomas Aquinas and Thomas à Kempis, the Book of Common Prayer and the 17th-century Anglican writers, as well as secular authors, both classical and English. Above all, though, they are deeply rooted in scripture; modern writer Leslie Griffiths identifies allusions to six Bible passages, from psalms, Gospels and epistles, in six lines of one hymn.[19]

John's preface to the 1780 Methodist hymn book, which became the definitive book for generations, says:

It… contain(s) all the important truths of our most holy religion, whether speculative or practical; yea, to illustrate them all, and to prove them both by Scripture and reason. The hymns… are carefully ranged under proper heads, according to the experience of real Christians. So that this book is in effect a little body of experimental and practical divinity.[20]

Modern writer Leslie Griffiths comments:

What the rosary, or pilgrimages, or the Spiritual Exercises, or the Prayer Book are as aids to spirituality in various Christian traditions, so hymns were (and are) to Methodists… Singing was the medium by which

Methodists learned and gave wing to their theology; it was as if the verses of Charles Wesley became the beads they fingered in their desire of 'perfecting holiness in the fear of God'.[21]

There were hymns for every occasion, from private prayer to the local class meeting and the annual conference. Their range of subjects, expressing rejoicing, penitence, suffering, intercession, and many that invite others to turn to Jesus, demonstrate 'Charles Wesley's capacity to describe, analyse and nourish the faith-experience of those who were coming in to the church'.[22] John, never one to leave anything unorganized, even provided rules for singing: 'Sing exactly, sing all, sing lustily, sing modestly (do not bawl), sing in time, sing spiritually.'[23]

Although hymns were used as part of private prayer, they were essentially for corporate use, as John's rules demonstrate—and they were meant to be enjoyed. The heart of the 1780 hymn book is for 'believers'. It is the largest section by far, and the largest subsection (there are ten of them) is for 'believers rejoicing'. As Leslie Griffiths says, 'Joy and happiness are the hallmarks of Charles Wesley's spirituality.'[24]

PRAYER

God of wisdom, fill me with your Spirit, making me joyful in you. Fill my heart with your praises, that I may give thanks to you at all times and for everything, in the name of our Lord Jesus Christ. Amen.

Saturday

A COVENANT OF THE HEART

The days are surely coming, says the Lord, when I will make a new covenant with the house of Israel and the house of Judah. It will not be like the covenant that I made with their ancestors when I took them by the hand to bring them out of the land of Egypt—a covenant that they broke, though I was their husband, says the Lord. But this is the covenant that I will make with the house of Israel after those days, says the Lord: I will put my law within them, and I will write it on their hearts; and I will be their God, and they shall be my people. No longer shall they teach one another, or say to each other, 'Know the Lord', for they shall all know me, from the least of them to the greatest, says the Lord; for I will forgive their iniquity, and remember their sin no more.
JEREMIAH 31:31–34

The discipline of the class system, with the expectation that every member was constantly struggling to become more like Christ, was a way of living out a desire that John Wesley had recognized well before his conversion in 1738. In the late 1720s, through reading the work of classical spiritual writers such as Thomas à Kempis, Jeremy Taylor and William Law, he came to be 'determined thro' his grace (the absolute necessity of which I was deeply sensible of) to be *all-devoted* to God, to give him *all* my soul, my body and my substance'.[25]

In 1755, the first covenant service was held, in the French Church at Spitalfields. Those present undertook a solemn covenant with God, and this became a regular part of Methodist church life. In 1780, John Wesley wrote a Covenant Service, along with instructions for its use, which was used for almost a century. It has been revised since then and is still in use, often at the beginning of a new year, and not only in the Methodist Church. It sums up in a moving and beautiful way the desire to give oneself to God that was at the heart of the Wesleys' spirituality, and the need that they recognized for each person to make such a commitment for themselves.

As with the whole history of covenant in the Bible, the people make their covenant in response to what God has already done and in recognition of his faithfulness. The covenants with Noah, with Abraham, with Isaac, with Jacob and with the people of Israel were often broken on the human side, but still God persevered. Today's passage from Jeremiah is often seen as a prophecy of the new covenant that God made in sending Jesus, offering to seal the covenant not with the blood of a sacrificial animal, but with his own lifeblood.

In Wesley's original service, the imagery of marriage is very strong and direct. 'O blessed Jesus, I come to you... and take you for my Head and Husband, for better, for worse, for richer, for poorer, for all times and conditions, to love, honour and obey you before all others, and this to the death.'[26] The modern service has the same total self-giving, but in rather different language. After adoration, thanksgiving and confession, and a time of silent prayer, the people pray:

I am no longer my own, but yours. Put me to what you will, rank me with whom you will; put me to doing, put me to suffering; let me be employed for you or laid aside for you, exalted for you or brought low for you; let me be full, let me be empty; let me have all things, let me have nothing; I freely and heartily yield all things to your pleasure and disposal. And now, O glorious and blessed God, Father, Son and Holy Spirit, you are mine, and I am yours. So be it. And the Covenant which I have made on earth, let it be ratified in heaven.[27]

As in marriage, this declaration of intent needs to be worked out each day; sometimes this will be easy and pleasurable, at other times difficult. In the modern Covenant service we hear, 'Christ has many services to be done; some are easy, others more difficult... In some we may please Christ and please ourselves; but there are others in which we cannot please Christ except by denying ourselves.'[28]

John Wesley could have lived a settled and easy life as a clergyman or academic, but the love of God compelled him to choose another way. He never had a settled home, and when he married, at the age of 48, it was disastrous. His wife did not share his passion for mission and left him three times, the final time for good.

Yet he, like his brother Charles, kept his covenant with God to the end. John died in 1791, surrounded by his disciples, having sung one of his brother's hymns, 'All glory to God in the sky', and a paraphrase of Psalm 146 by Isaac Watts, 'I'll praise my Maker while I've breath; And when my voice is lost in death, Praise shall employ my nobler powers.'[29] His last words were, 'The best of all is, God is with us.'

PRAYER

Faithful God, you keep your covenant with your people through all generations. Give me an answering faithfulness in my service of you, joy in praising you, peace in obeying you, and strength to choose your will now and every day. Amen.

SING TO THE LORD

It has famously been said that 'Methodism was born in song'. John Wesley, in the preface he wrote to the 1780 hymn book, said, 'I would recommend it to every truly pious reader: as a means of raising or quickening the spirit of devotion, of confirming his faith, of enlivening his hope, and of kindling and increasing his love to God and man.'[30]

Spend some time this week considering which hymns or spiritual songs do this for you, and then include some of them in your times of prayer. You don't need to be a good singer; only God will be listening and he made your body and soul, including your voice.

You might want to compile your own small collection of favourite hymns and songs to keep with whatever books of prayers you regularly use, so that music and singing can become a regular part of your prayer.

Charles and John didn't have the luxury of recorded music, but we do, and you might like also to compile a selection of recorded music that raises your heart and mind to God and moves you to worship. Use it when devotion is hard to kindle, but don't make it a substitute for raising your own voice to God in praise.

GET TO GRIPS WITH GRACE

Make a theological study of grace. Begin by identifying key passages in the Bible, using a concordance. Then study these passages with the help of commentaries. You may find it helpful to make a note of ideas that particularly strike you, and any that puzzle you or with which you disagree. Dictionaries of theology will give you an overview of the subject and suggest ways to follow up particular lines of thought and enquiry.

Reflect too on times in your life when you have been particularly aware of God's grace working in you. You may have been aware of it at the time, or it may be only in hindsight that you can see it. These are the converting times in our lives, when God is especially at work. But his grace is also available every day, in the very ordinary times, as we seek to grow in holiness.

MAKE A COVENANT WITH GOD

This might be a project to begin now and continue through the rest of Lent. Look at the covenants God makes in the Bible, and the words of the Methodist Covenant Service, and consider what you would include in your own personal covenant with God. What can you offer? What would you ask?

Note down ideas as they come to you, and work towards writing your own personal covenant and God's response to it. You might want to share it with a spiritual guide if you have one, or with a trusted friend. As you celebrate Easter, use your covenant as a way of making a new commitment to God in the light of all you have learnt this Lent.

John Donne

Sunday

A PASSIONATE MAN

Mary stood weeping outside the tomb. As she wept, she bent over to look into the tomb; and she saw two angels in white, sitting where the body of Jesus had been lying, one at the head and the other at the feet. They said to her, 'Woman, why are you weeping?' She said to them, 'They have taken away my Lord, and I do not know where they have laid him.' When she had said this, she turned round and saw Jesus standing there, but she did not know that it was Jesus. Jesus said to her, 'Woman, why are you weeping? For whom are you looking?' Supposing him to be the gardener, she said to him, 'Sir, if you have carried him away, tell me where you have laid him, and I will take him away.' Jesus said to her, 'Mary!' She turned and said to him in Hebrew, 'Rabbouni!' (which means Teacher).

JOHN 20:11–16

Like the Wesley brothers, John Donne, our companion for this week, wrote widely. Unlike them, he is best known for his poetry. He left no journals of his spiritual experience, but he did write some meditations and many sermons. It is from the poems in particular, however, that we can get a sense of what kind of man he was.

John Donne was born in a time of religious turmoil. The 16th century saw the Reformation taking place in England, when the main religion of the country changed from the Catholic faith to a Protestant one. The change was not without difficulty and there were martyrs on both sides. Donne was born in 1572, in the reign of Elizabeth I, into a Catholic family. One of his uncles was the leader of a secret Jesuit mission to England, and when Donne was 21, one of his brothers, Henry, just a year younger than John, died in Newgate prison in London, where he had been sent for the crime of sheltering a Catholic priest. John's mother was a descendant of Thomas More, who had been executed in the reign of Henry VIII for refusing to co-operate in the first of the king's many divorces.

For Donne's family, then, faith was literally a matter of life and death, and perhaps this contributed to his passionate character. As a young man, his passion was not directed towards God, but towards women. By the time he reached his 20s, in the last decade of the century, he was no longer a convinced Catholic, and in 1596 and 1597 he took part in two naval expeditions against the Spaniards, perhaps hoping to convince others of his patriotism and his adherence to the Protestant faith, a move that would help his career.

Donne went to Oxford University, and then returned to London to study law. It was during this time that he began to write poetry, both satires on contemporary society and love poetry. He was very secretive about this writing, and gave copies only to a few trusted friends, making them promise not to pass them on. In a letter of around 1600, he wrote, 'Except I receive by your next letter an assurance upon the religion of your friendship that no copy shall be taken for any respect of these or any other my compositions sent to you, I shall sin against my conscience if I send you any more.'[1]

His love poems are extraordinarily erotic, although this is sometimes disguised by the complexity of the language and thought. An early poem, 'To his mistress going to bed', contains these lines, which leave little to the imagination:

Licence my roving hands, and let them go
Behind, before, above, between, below.
O my America, my new found land,
My kingdom, safeliest when with one man manned...[2]

Donne's passionate nature soon got him into trouble. In 1601 he married, in secret, the niece of his employer, Sir Thomas Egerton, which led to his dismissal from his post as secretary and, in reality, to the end of his career. He spent the next 13 years without regular work, depending on the kindness of friends to support his growing family. He continued to write, and produced the *Songs and Sonnets* that contain some of his best love poetry.

In 1615, encouraged by King James I, he was ordained in the Church of England, and was appointed as a royal chaplain. Two years later his wife died, and in 1621 Donne was made Dean of St Paul's, a post he held for ten years until his death on 31 March 1631.

The passion that Donne had expressed for women as a young man gradually turned to a passion for God, and his later poems, in particular the *Holy Sonnets*, express it powerfully. Wherever his passion led him, like Mary Magdalene, he threw himself totally into it. In a sermon preached in 1628, again like Mary Magdalene, he desires to be with Christ wherever it takes him.

He that will die with Christ upon Good Friday, must hear his own bell toll all Lent; he that will be partaker of his passion at last, must conform himself to his discipline of prayer and fasting before... We must be in his grave, before we come to his resurrection, and we must be in his death-bed before we come to his grave.[3]

PRAYER

God of passion, may I turn all my passion towards you this Lent. Make me willing to follow you wherever it may take me, to the cross, to the grave, and to the resurrection. Amen.

Monday

A LOVING GOD

'For God so loved the world that he gave his only Son, so that everyone who believes in him may not perish but may have eternal life.'

JOHN 3:16

See what love the Father has given us, that we should be called children of God; and that is what we are. The reason the world does not know us is that it did not know him. Beloved, we are God's children now; what we will be has not yet been revealed.

1 JOHN 3:1–2a

Donne's struggles with his own faith mirrored those of the age in which he lived. He had renounced the Catholic faith of his up-bringing, it seems, in the hope of making a good career for himself, only to wreck his chances by his marriage. His *Songs and Sonnets*, written during his marriage, although they are fundamentally love poems, use much religious imagery, and it is Catholic, not Protest-ant. He writes of angels and saints and relics, and occasionally, glancingly, of being apostate. We have no record of how his family and friends reacted to his abandonment of his family faith, but some would have believed (and maybe sometimes he did himself) that he had chosen eternal damnation by abandoning the true faith.

So it is not surprising that, certainly in his poetry, including his overtly religious poetry, Donne seems much more familiar with God's absence than with his presence. Nearly all his religious poems are poems of struggle, not of calm assurance, and perhaps this is one reason why he remains so popular. We all have times when our faith is hanging by a thread; we wonder if God has abandoned us, or what we have done wrong to be feeling so far from him. In these times, Donne's poems can speak to us and for us.

Yet Donne held together this doubt and struggle with a faith that God's passion for him, and for all his people, was far stronger than his for God. He had studied theology from the age of 19, and knew the words of the Gospels and the epistles that spoke of God's great love for his world. He would have been aware of the theological controversies of the Reformation, and the recovery of the belief in salvation by faith alone which was one of the great gifts of the reformed theologians.

All who preach know how often they preach what they them-selves need to hear, what they themselves are preoccupied with, and Donne was probably no different. So when we find him preaching in 1617 on the theme 'Salvation sure', we can hope that he was listening to his own words and being comforted by them.

What soul among us shall doubt, that when God hath such an abundant, and infinite treasure, as the merit and passion of Christ Jesus, sufficient to save millions of worlds… when God hath a kingdom so large, as that nothing limits it… what soul amongst us shall doubt, but that he that hath thus much, and loves thus much, will not deny her a portion in the blood of Christ or a room in the kingdom of heaven?[4]

In Holy Sonnet 13, 'Thou hast made me, and shall thy work decay?', Donne speaks of his heart as 'iron' that God, like a magnet, will draw to himself. Perhaps he was remembering Jesus' words in John 12:32: 'And I, when I am lifted up from the earth, will draw all people to myself.'

Donne came to see that God's mercy was always present, always available and always overflowing. As the apostle John says, 'We are God's children now', and what parent would not give their chil-dren what they ask? (Luke 11:10–13). In a sermon preached on

Christmas Day 1624, Donne uses all the powers at his disposal to convince his hearers that God's passion for them is rich and overflowing.

God made sun and moon to distinguish seasons, and day, and night, and we cannot have the fruits of the earth but in their seasons: But God hath made no decree to distinguish the seasons of his mercies; in paradise, the fruits were ripe, the first minute, and in heaven it is always autumn, his mercies are ever in their maturity… He brought light out of darkness, not out of a lesser light; he can bring thy summer out of winter, though thou have no spring; though in the ways of fortune, or understanding, or conscience, thou have been benighted till now, wintered and frozen, clouded and eclipsed, damped and benumbed, smothered and stupified till now, now God comes to thee, not as in the dawning of the day, not as in the bud of the spring, but as the sun at noon… as the sheaves in harvest… all occasions invite his mercies, and all times are his seasons.[5]

Donne had certainly been benighted in 'the ways of fortune… or conscience' but his God had come to him, drawing him as irresistibly as a magnet draws iron, and convincing him that despite his vacillations of faith and his disreputable youth, he was loved and saved by God's grace. It was a conviction that would sustain him as he struggled with sin and sickness and the fear of death, and it is a conviction that we need as we move deeper into the passion of Christ.

PRAYER

God of love, come to me. Come to me in my perplexities and doubts, in my darkness and numbness, and help me to know myself as your child now, held safe in your mercy for ever. Amen.

Tuesday

A CONTRITE HEART

Have mercy on me, O God, according to your steadfast love; according to your abundant mercy blot out my transgressions. Wash me thoroughly from my iniquity, and cleanse me from my sin. For I know my transgressions, and my sin is ever before me. Against you, you alone, have I sinned, and done what is evil in your sight, so that you are justified in your sentence and blameless when you pass judgment. Indeed, I was born guilty, a sinner when my mother conceived me…

Create in me a clean heart, O God, and put a new and right spirit within me…

For you have no delight in sacrifice; if I were to give a burnt-offering, you would not be pleased. The sacrifice acceptable to God is a broken spirit; a broken and contrite heart, O God, you will not despise.

PSALM 51:1–5, 10, 16–17

Sin loomed large in John Donne's view of himself. His passionate nature had led him into much that he felt had separated him from God, so he was passionately convinced of his need for God's forgiveness and grace. He wrote:

If I confess to thee the sins of my youth, wilt thou ask me if I know what those sins were? I know them not so well as to name them all, nor am sure to live hours enough to name them all (for I did them then, faster than I can speak them now, when every thing that I did, conduced to some sin), but I know them so well, as to know, that nothing but thy mercy is so infinite as they.[6]

We do not know what sins Donne was thinking of when he wrote this passage, but his early love poems give us an indication that he probably did not keep the church's rules on sex outside marriage. His two naval expeditions to Spain may have involved violence or even killing of the hated enemy. Nevertheless, he is eloquent that it is not only these large and obvious sins that cut us off from God. Sin is as much an attitude as it is particular actions.

In a sermon from 1617, he speaks of 'a heart of sin, which must be cast up; for whilst the heart is under the habits of sin, we are not only sinful, but we are all sin; as it is truly said, that land overflow'd with sea, is all sea.'[7] So he and we can pray, 'Create in me a clean heart, and put a new and right spirit within me.'

In a marvellous image, Donne gives us a picture of the work that must be done in order to obtain this pure heart.

So also must he that affects this pureness of heart, and studies the preserving of it, sweep down every cobweb that hangs about it. Scurrile and obscene language; yea, misinterpretable words, such as may bear an ill sense... and all such little entanglings, which though he think too weak to hold him, yet they foul him.[8]

The small sins, which we may think go unnoticed and do not really affect us, are evidence of an attitude of heart that damages our walk with God. They mount up until there are as many 'lascivious glances as shall make up an adultery, as many covetous wishes as shall make up a robbery, as many angry words as shall make up a murder; and thou shalt have dropped and crumbled away thy soul, with as much irrecoverableness, as if thou hadst poured it out all at once'.[9] This concern to root out the attitudes that lead to sin, as well as sin itself, stems from Jesus' own teaching (Matthew 5:21–22, 27–28).

What is the answer? The contrite heart of the psalmist, the

acknowledgment of transgression and sin, will bring us to the joy of salvation. Donne knew the subtle arguments of some theologians that sin, along with sickness and death, had no reality because they had not been created by God. He knew also that, in reality, we fear sickness and death and their effects on us, and so we should also fear sin. Far from denying its reality, we must own it, and in that owning will be the beginning of hope and forgiveness. 'But except we do come to say, Our sins are ours, God will never cut up that root in us, God will never blot out the memory in himself, of those sins. Nothing can make them none of ours, but the avowing of them, the confessing of them to be ours.' There is a wonderful paradox here: 'by that confessing and appropriating of those sins to my self, they are made the sins of him, who hath suffered enough for all, my blessed Lord and Saviour, Christ Jesus'.[10]

God's mercy and love were, after all, great enough to wash away Donne's sins, and to deliver his soul from death.

PRAYER

God of sinners, I acknowledge my sinfulness, in attitude and action, and especially… (name any sin of which you are particularly conscious at present). In your mercy forgive me, through the death and resurrection of your beloved Son and my Lord, Jesus Christ. Amen.

Wednesday

IN SICKNESS AND IN HEALTH

Are any among you suffering? They should pray. Are any cheerful? They should sing songs of praise. Are any among you sick? They should call for the elders of the church and have them pray over them, anointing them with oil in the name of the Lord. The prayer of faith will save the sick, and the Lord will raise them up; and anyone who has committed sins will be forgiven. Therefore confess your sins to one another, and pray for one another, so that you may be healed.

JAMES 5:13–16a

Some theologians may have denied the ultimate reality of sickness, because it had not been created by God, but Donne, like James in his epistle, knew that sickness was real and painful. In common with many of his time, he saw sin as the primary cause of sickness, but not necessarily the particular sin of a particular person. Rather, it was part of the fallen condition of humankind.

Donne's father had died when he was only four years old; the following year his elder sister Elizabeth died, and in 1581 his two youngest siblings, Mary and Katherine. His stepfather died when he was 16, and, as we already know, his younger brother Henry died when Donne was 21. His own family, with his wife Ann, was not exempt from sickness and death. They had ten children born alive, with two stillborn; of these, three died in childhood, and Lucy, his fourth child and second daughter, died at the age of 19. Ann herself died in 1617, after giving birth to their second stillborn child.

Donne himself suffered various bouts of illness during his life, including neuritis in the winter of 1608/9, an eye disease that left him almost blind for a time in autumn 1613, a relapsing fever in the autumn of 1623, and his final illness, possibly consumption, which began in August 1630 and continued until his death at the end of March 1631. His mother had died in January of that year.

Donne's illness of 1623, which almost killed him, led to his *Devotions upon Emergent Occasions*, a series of meditations and prayers in which he reflects on sickness and death. At the very start, he writes of how suddenly illness can come upon us, despite all our precautions. In our health-conscious days, when we may come to believe that we can prevent any illness by taking enough care, this is a salutary reminder.

Variable, and therefore miserable condition of man; this minute I was well, and am ill, this minute. I am surprised with a sudden change, and alteration to worse, and can impute it to no cause, nor call it by any name. We study health, and we deliberate upon our meats, and drink, and air, and exercise, and we hew and polish every stone that goes to that building; and so our health is a long and regular work: but in a minute a cannon batters all, overthrows all, demolishes all; a sickness unprevented for all our diligence, unsuspected for all our curiosity; nay undeserved, if we consider only disorder, summons us, seizes us, possesses us, destroys us in an instant.[11]

As we can see from this extract, Donne's writing is at the same time poetic, yet very acute about the reality of illness. In the prayer of chapter XV, he reflects on the insomnia that his illness has brought, and the way in which, lying awake, he is very much aware of his sinfulness, and anxious lest his illness lead him into more sin. Anyone who has lain awake night after night through pain or other effects of illness will sympathize with him. Like the apostle James, he turns to prayer.

O eternal and most gracious God, who art able to make, and dost make, the sick bed of thy servants chapels of ease to them, and the dreams of thy servants prayers and meditations upon thee, let not this continual watchfulness of mine, this inability to sleep, which thou hast laid upon me, be any disquiet or discomfort to me, but rather an argument, that thou wouldst not have me sleep in thy presence.

He prays to be preserved from that compulsive ruminating on the meaning of every twinge and symptom: 'What it may indicate or signify concerning the state of my body, let them consider to whom that consideration belongs.'[12]

Donne is realistic: he knows that sickness will, in the end, lead to death. In one of his sonnets, he calls it 'sickness, death's herald, and champion'.[13] But he knows also that death will not have the final word, and so even in his sickness he continues to look to God, and to expect that here too God will be present and working.

PRAYER

God of my life and death, in health make me grateful, and in sickness make me trusting. My days are in your hand, and whether they be short or long, your will be done and your name be glorified in my living and in my dying. Amen.

Thursday

THE FEAR OF DEATH

Jesus came out and went, as was his custom, to the Mount of Olives; and the disciples followed him. When he reached the place, he said to them, 'Pray that you may not come into the time of trial.' Then he withdrew from them about a stone's throw, knelt down, and prayed, 'Father, if you are willing, remove this cup from me; yet, not my will but yours be done.' ... When he got up from prayer, he came to the disciples and found them sleeping because of grief, and he said to them, 'Why are you sleeping? Get up and pray that you may not come into the time of trial.'

LUKE 22:39–42, 45–46

Donne knew through faith that death would not have the last word, but its voice was loud in his ears. The fear of death, and an awareness of the inevitability of death, is a thread running through much of his writing. Perhaps he found some comfort in this story of Jesus' prayer on the Mount of Olives. Certainly, even non-believers can find it powerful: 'Though a passionate atheist, Professor Nussbaum concedes that Christianity is made immeasurably more powerful by imagining a God who is also fully human. Christ's victory is not guaranteed in advance. In Gethsemane, Christ's love and courage coincide with a moment of maximum risk.'[14] One could add, of fear. Jesus was not exempt from the human fear of extinction and of the process of dying.

Donne was acutely aware of the brevity of life, and seems to have always felt that death was near, perhaps just round the next corner.

'We are all conceived in close prison; in our mother's wombs, we are close prisoners all; when we are born, we are born but to the liberty of the house; prisoners still, though within larger walls; and then all our life is but a going out to the place of execution, to death.'[15]

Death was, as it still is, a great leveller. No money or status or power can stave off death for ever, although they may keep it at bay for a time, or make its coming and its endurance easier.

It comes equally to us all, and makes us all equal when it comes. The ashes of an oak in the chimney, are no epitaph of that oak, to tell me how high or how large that was; It tells me not what flock it sheltered while it stood, nor what men it hurt when it fell.[16]

Donne goes on to say that the dust of a wretch will get in your eye in the same way as the dust of a prince, and that the man sweeping out the dust of the churchyard from the church cannot distinguish the dust of one from another. Donne portrays the reality of death starkly, and it was this reality that Jesus faced in Gethsemane, so that in our fear of death we may know that we are not alone.

In the reflections that he wrote after his serious illness of 1623, Donne could sometimes look more calmly upon death. As he lay in bed listening to the bells tolling for others who were dying or dead, he could even see death as 'a preferment', as a translation to something better, to which he, as a member of humankind, should aspire. 'But as when men see many of their own professions preferred, it ministers a hope that that may light upon them; so when these hourly bells tell me of so many funerals of men like me, it presents, if not a desire that it may, yet a comfort whensoever mine shall come.'[17]

It is the common lot of humankind to die, but as a Christian, Donne knows that in dying he will not fall out of God's hand. As in baptism he was connected to Christ, the head of the body, so in death he will not be separated from him. So the death of anyone, who is a part of the body, affects him: 'Any man's death diminishes me, because I am involved in mankind, and therefore never send to know for whom the bell tolls; it tolls for thee.'[18] Used rightly, this kind of reflection can lead us closer to God.

Neither can we call this a begging of misery, or a borrowing of misery, as though we were not miserable enough of ourselves... Tribulation is treasure in the nature of it, but it is not current money in the use of it, except we get nearer and nearer our home, heaven, by it. Another man may be sick too... and this affliction may lie in his bowels, as gold in a mine, and be of no use to him; but this bell, that tells me of his affliction, digs out and applies that gold to me, if by this consideration of another's danger I take mine own into contemplation, and so secure myself, by making my course to my God, who is our only security.[19]

PRAYER

Lord Jesus Christ, thank you that you knew the fear of death, so that I may not be alone in my fear. Thank you that you overcame the fear of death, so that I may not be overcome. Amen.

Friday

DEATH SHALL DIE

Now if Christ is proclaimed as raised from the dead, how can some of you say there is no resurrection of the dead? If there is no resurrection of the dead, then Christ has not been raised; and if Christ has not been raised, then our proclamation has been in vain and your faith has been in vain...

But in fact Christ has been raised from the dead, the first fruits of those who have died. For since death came through a human being, the resurrection of the dead has also come through a human being; for as all die in Adam, so all will be made alive in Christ. But each in his own order: Christ the first fruits, then at his coming those who belong to Christ. Then comes the end, when he hands over the kingdom to God the Father, after he has destroyed every ruler and every authority and power. For he must reign until he has put all his enemies under his feet. The last enemy to be destroyed is death.

1 CORINTHIANS 15:12–14, 20–26

If Donne wrote vividly of the reality of death and the natural human fear of it, he wrote equally vividly of the hope of resurrection, resting on the resurrection of Christ. He imagined himself, at the resurrection of the body, saying to Christ, 'I am of the same stuff as you, body and body, flesh and flesh, and therefore let me sit down with you, at the right hand of the Father'[20] because death, the last enemy, has been destroyed in Christ's death.

Because the new life of the resurrection is indeed new life, it is hard to describe, hard to imagine. Paul uses much of the long 15th chapter of his first letter to the Corinthians trying to explain what the resurrection will be like, and to answer some of the Corinthians' questions. He uses the image of the seed, which must die in order to come to new life. The new life is contained in the seed that is sown, but may look very different from the seed when it grows (1 Corinthians 15:36–38).

Donne too struggled to find language to describe the resurrection. As a former librarian, I particularly enjoy his image of humankind as one volume with one author. When someone dies, their chapter 'is not torn out of the book, but translated into a better language'. Various translators are employed by God—age, sickness, war, justice—'but God's hand is in every translation, and his hand shall bind up all our scattered leaves again, for that library where every book shall lie open to one another'.[21]

In one of his sermons, Donne uses another vivid image. He sees himself as money, given in taxes to the king, and so becoming part of the royal exchequer: 'So this body... being given in subsidy, as a contribution to the glory of my God, in the grave, becomes a part of God's Exchequer.'[22] In the same sermon, he goes on to make an important point, one that is very biblical but is often forgotten today. The angels, he says, shall rejoice 'when they shall see me in my soul, to have all that they have, and in my body, to have that that they have not'.[23]

The Christian doctrine of the resurrection is a very earthy and physical one. We will not be disembodied spirits, but whole people, body and soul; changed indeed, no longer perishable and mortal but imperishable and immortal (1 Corinthians 15:53). Donne knew that this was a difficult thing to believe. In another sermon, he says that the immortality of the soul is easy to believe in, but the immortality of the body can only be believed by faith. He lists some of the difficulties that will be raised against this belief. How can a body, burnt a thousand years ago, ash scattered in wrinkles and furrows of the earth, be brought together again? How can a bone shattered by shot be put back together? How can a body that lost an arm in Europe and a leg in Asia be reassembled?

Only by God's power, he says. God knows 'in what part of the world every grain of every man's dust lies; and… he whispers, he hisses, he beckons for the bodies of his saints, and in the twinkling of an eye, that body that was scattered over all the elements, is sat down at the right hand of God, in a glorious resurrection.'[24]

No wonder he could write, in one of his most famous sonnets:

Death be not proud…
One short sleep past, we wake eternally,
And death shall be no more. Death, thou shalt die.[25]

PRAYER

God of resurrection, strengthen my faith in the wonders of the resurrection, new life for body and soul. Amen.

Saturday

A MIND TRANSFORMED

Therefore prepare your minds for action; discipline yourselves; set all your hope on the grace that Jesus Christ will bring you when he is revealed. Like obedient children, do not be conformed to the desires that you formerly had in ignorance. Instead, as he who called you is holy, be holy yourselves in all your conduct; for it is written, 'You shall be holy, for I am holy.'

1 PETER 1:13–16

In heaven, Donne believed, it is not only our bodies that will be transformed, but also our minds. In an Easter sermon, he preached that we would no longer need to move from one author to another, from one subject to another, but 'God shall create us all doctors in a minute'.[26]

Donne himself seemed to have little need of such a transformation: he was formidably learned and intelligent, and both his poetry and his prose demonstrate great learning and skill in deploying it. For much of his life, he rose at four in the morning and studied until ten. Izaak Walton, who wrote a brief life of Donne in 1656, 25 years after his death, says that particularly after his ordination he was constantly studying in preparing his sermons, which show evidence of very wide reading. Walton says that he left notes, abridged and analysed, of the work of 1400 authors. In his sermons he often refers to what 'the schoolmen' say—that is, the medieval scholastic theologians such as Thomas Aquinas. He quotes extensively from the Bible, and knew many languages, both ancient and modern.

Even so, he knew that reason alone was not enough. The mind had to be used well in order to be a means of serving God: 'The common light of reason illumines us all; but one employs this light upon the searching of impertinent vanities, another by a better use of the same light, finds out the mysteries of religion.'[27] He goes on to give examples. Some have invented useful things, such as printing, which has helped the whole world to communicate with each other and share their inventions, knowledge, and trade; and artillery, which has saved lives by shortening wars. Others have used their reason to find ways of profiting from others' weaknesses, or to seduce women more efficiently. (Perhaps he spoke from experience on this last score!)

Donne's poetry and his prose are complex, often hard to understand at first. He weaves great nets of language and creates a world of allusions and illusions, in which things are often not what they seem at first. Yet he is worth struggling with. He knew his own complexities, his mixed motives and apparently contradictory desires and feelings, and sought to include them all in his writing.

A modern writer says of him:

Donne gave to the emergent tradition of Anglican poetics a certain psychological realism, a willingness to look directly at our complex emotional and intellectual lives without reducing them to mere principles of theory, an insistence on our need for God's grace and its power to produce hope and connection where we could not produce it for ourselves. Donne had a strong comprehension of how deep a need this is. He seems to have sensed how much darkness is possible in the human soul as well as how much delight we can encompass.[28]

This realism marked the end of Donne's life too. As we have seen, his last illness lasted many months. On 13 December 1630, he made his will. Despite great weakness, he insisted on continuing to preach on certain occasions. As he drew closer to death, one of his friends encouraged him to have a monument made for his grave, but left the design of it to Donne. He asked a painter to come to him and, when the artist arrived, took off all his clothes, wrapped himself in a winding sheet, as if already dead, and stood upon an urn. The painter drew him, and Donne kept the picture beside his bed, meditating on it until his death on 31 March 1631. After his death, a white marble monument was carved from this picture, and it can still be seen in St Paul's Cathedral in London, having survived the Great Fire of 1666.

Donne's desires, always strong, had brought him to a great love of God and a great trust in him. He sought out the truth with all his mind, and gave all his considerable energies to communicating it to others. Heart and mind came together to create a guide who seems still contemporary, as he wrestled with all the glorious complexities of human existence in the light of divine love.

PRAYER

Lord, make me obedient to the truth of your word, and diligent in seeking it out with all my mind and heart and strength. Amen.

USE YOUR MIND

How do you use your mind in the exercise of your faith? Is it the place in which you will naturally start when grappling with some problem, or is it your last resort when all else fails? Do you make decisions on the basis of the facts and on your thought-through conclusions; or on the basis of what feels right?

Both can be legitimate, but it can be useful at times to try to work with your weaker sides. So if you usually work from your feelings, try this week to engage your mind more, to set aside, at least for a time, your instinctive, gut reaction, your felt response, to situations and questions, and to think them through instead.

Consider also the place of study in your walk with God. Do you put aside time to study the Bible? Do you grapple with theological language and ideas, trying to come to a greater understanding of them? Do you engage with ethical quandaries and controversial issues in the church, reading the evidence and the arguments on both sides of the question? Or are you tempted to leave this work to others, to go along with the theology, biblical interpretation, and ethics of those around you?

WRITE

Spend some time this week writing. Give thanks to God for the gift of language, for all it can do, for the ways in which we can use it to communicate with each other, with ourselves, and with God. Here are just a few ideas:

- Keep a journal. Spend a few minutes each day noting down what has struck you during the day, what you want to remember, anything you have read that has made an impact, subjects for prayer—whatever you like.

- Write a poem. You don't have to show it to anyone. Use language in unusual and creative ways to reflect on your feelings. You may surprise yourself with the images you find.

- Record your studies. If you studied grace last week, or have taken up one of the ideas from 'Use your mind', write down what you've come to understand better, what you still don't understand, and what you found helpful and unhelpful in your reading.

- Write a letter to God. Be honest and say what you really want to say. Don't worry if you seem to contradict yourself. Like all relationships, our relationship with God has both light and darkness in it, and it is good to acknowledge both sides.

BE PASSIONATE

What are you really passionate about? You can probably tell by looking at how you choose to spend your time, your energy and your money. You can't usually be passionate in the abstract or in theory. If someone tells you that they are passionate about music, you would think it was very odd if they went on to say that they hardly ever listened to music or went to concerts.

What does this reflection tell you about your feelings towards God? How might you nurture a passion for God in practical and concrete ways? You can draw lessons from the other relationships in your life. How do you show your love for your partner, parents, children, friends? How might these ways translate into love for God?

— HOLY WEEK —

Julian of Norwich

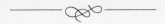

Palm Sunday

OUR COURTEOUS LORD

When they had come near Jerusalem and had reached Bethphage, at the Mount of Olives, Jesus sent two disciples, saying to them, 'Go into the village ahead of you, and immediately you will find a donkey tied, and a colt with her; untie them and bring them to me. If anyone says anything to you, just say this, "The Lord needs them." And he will send them immediately.' This took place to fulfil what had been spoken through the prophet, saying, 'Tell the daughter of Zion, Look, your king is coming to you, humble, and mounted on a donkey, and on a colt, the foal of a donkey.' The disciples went and did as Jesus had directed them; they brought the donkey and the colt, and put their cloaks on them, and he sat on them.

MATTHEW 21:1–7

Our companion for this final week is one of my personal favourites; indeed, I added her name to my own when I joined my community. In my enthusiasm I find myself in good company: Thomas Merton, the famous 20th-century Cistercian monk, and another of my personal favourites, wrote of her in the early 1960s:

Julian is without doubt one of the most wonderful of all Christian voices. She gets greater and greater in my eyes as I grow older and whereas in the old days I used to be crazy about St John of the Cross, I would not exchange him now for Julian if you gave me the world and the Indies and all the Spanish mystics rolled up in one bundle.[1]

Bishop John Robinson described her theology as 'astonishingly whole and extraordinarily modern'.[2]

Julian herself would have refused these compliments. Although she was the first woman to write a book in English, she wrote of herself as 'ignorant, weak and frail'. Yet she cannot deny what she has experienced: 'I know what I am saying: I have been shown it by the sovereign teacher.'[3]

What Julian had been shown came to her in a series of visions during a serious illness at the age of 30. At some point—perhaps after the visions, perhaps before—she chose to become a recluse, living a solitary life next to the church of St Julian in Norwich, from which she takes her name. Like the author of *The Cloud of Unknowing*, we know very little about her, and nearly all that we do know comes from the two versions of the *Revelations of Divine Love* that she wrote. The first and shorter one was written soon after her visions, the longer after many years of reflection and prayer.

Julian wrote her books not to glorify herself but to point her readers to God: 'I entreat you... to disregard the wretched sinful creature to whom this vision was shown; and firmly, wisely, lovingly and meekly behold God who, in his courteous love and endless goodness, would show it generally as a comfort to us all.'[4]

'Courteous' is one of Julian's favourite words to describe God, and it is closely allied in her mind to humility. The God who emptied himself (Philippians 2:5–11) and took on our human nature comes to each of us humbly, as he arrived in Jerusalem. He is infinitely patient, always inviting us to a closer relationship, always waiting for us to respond. His love is greater than our sin: Julian writes, 'His love excuses us. In his great courtesy he overlooks the blame, and regards us with sympathy and pity, children both innocent and loved.'[5]

We, for our part, should return this courteous, sensitive love. For Julian, this means not seeking to understand everything now; there are things that are 'our Lord's own private matter'.[6] It is not wrong, however, to ask for enlightenment, although we may not receive an answer. Julian herself worked with her revelations for many years, praying with them and asking God to make clear to her what was not clear. The fruits of this work are to be found in the longer text of the *Revelations*, which is three and a half times as long as the original shorter text. At one point in this process, she was told to look carefully at every detail of a particular revelation, and perhaps this is a good message for us as we enter Holy Week. The Bible stories are very familiar, and it is easy to think that we have already exhausted their meaning and to pass over them swiftly. Maybe, instead, we should persevere in praying with them, reflecting on their every detail and asking God to reveal what more he has to show us.

PRAYER

Courteous and humble Lord, give me patience and perseverance as I follow you this week on the way of the cross. Open my eyes to your revelations of love in all that I hear and see, and make me willing also to live with what I don't yet understand. Amen.

Monday

JESUS OUR MOTHER

Rejoice with Jerusalem, and be glad for her, all you who love her; rejoice with her in joy, all you who mourn over her—that you may nurse and be satisfied from her consoling breast; that you may drink deeply with delight from her glorious bosom. For thus says the Lord: I will extend prosperity to her like a river, and the wealth of the nations like an overflowing stream; and you shall nurse and be carried on her arm, and dandled on her knees. As a mother comforts her child, so I will comfort you; you shall be comforted in Jerusalem.
ISAIAH 66:10–13

'Jerusalem, Jerusalem, the city that kills the prophets and stones those who are sent to it! How often have I desired to gather your children together as a hen gathers her brood under her wings, and you were not willing!'
MATTHEW 23:37

Given her description of us as 'children both innocent and loved', it is not surprising that Julian moves naturally into describing Jesus as our mother. It is an image that appears occasionally in the Bible, and was not unknown in Christian spirituality, especially in the early centuries and among the Greek Fathers. Anselm revived it in the eleventh century, and the twelfth-century Cistercian writers, including Aelred, also used it. There is no proof that Julian knew these works, but they were widely available and influential, and it is likely that she had heard or read some of them at least.

Julian uses this image on a number of different levels, and moves from better-known uses of the image to more original ones. The church has traditionally been seen as mother, and Julian uses this image: 'And for now, I yield myself to my mother holy Church, as any simple child should.'[7]

Mary, because she is the mother of Christ, in whom we are included, is also our mother: 'For she who is mother of the Saviour is mother of all who will be saved in our Saviour. And our Saviour is our true Mother in whom we are endlessly born.'[8] Julian moves quite easily from the thought of Mary as our mother to Jesus as even more our mother, as our true Mother.

In this use of the image, she draws from the work of a natural mother, who knows the needs of her children and treats them appropriately, but always in love: 'The kind, loving mother who knows and understands the needs of her child protects it most tenderly in keeping with the nature and character of motherhood. As it grows older she changes her treatment, but not her love.'[9] And it is right that we should act towards Jesus as we would towards our own mother, not running away when things go wrong, but following 'our childish nature; for when a child is upset or frightened it runs quickly to its mother with all its might'.[10]

Left at this level, it could seem a nice, rather sentimental picture of an idealized mother, always caring, always loving. In fact, though, the image goes much deeper. It is found only in the later Long Text, and so it was the fruit of much reflection and meditation on Julian's part. Although the image is not original to her, she 'developed this conception into a doctrine not found before in such fulness, and made it a pillar of her teaching on the spiritual life'.[11] She did this by incorporating it into her theology of the Trinity: 'Thus in our creation God almighty is our natural father, and God all-wisdom our natural mother, who together with the love and goodness of the holy ghost are all one God, one lord.'[12]

In chapters 58—63 of the Long Text of the Revelations, Julian develops this basic insight with great richness and theological skill, but always holding together the essential unity of the Trinity. At various points, she describes the persons of the trinity as Father, Mother, Lord; as power, wisdom, goodness; as nature, mercy, grace; and as protection, restoration, fulfilment. She also relates the three persons to three stages in our lives, which Beer identifies as 'natural being (created before time by the father); growth (which occurs during our life on earth); and perfection (brought about by the Holy Spirit)'.[13] It is the second stage which is most difficult, and it is there that our mother Jesus guides and nurtures us. Not only that; he also brings us to birth through his passion, as our earthly mothers brought us to birth in labour. They fed us with their milk, but he feeds us with his own body and blood in the Eucharist.

For Julian, this image is not primarily about gender (although she often refers to Jesus as mother, she never uses the word 'she' of him) but about relationship. Although we know next to nothing of Julian's relationship with her own mother, we can perhaps believe that it was good, warm and caring, giving her a starting point for the meditations that led to such a striking and original development in her thought, and a gift for us today in our own relationship with God, who is Father, Mother, and Lord.

PRAYER

God, Holy Trinity, Father, Mother, Lord, lead me more deeply into all the richness of your being. Open my eyes and my heart to the depths of your love, and bring me to new birth in your love. Amen.

Tuesday

FALLING AND RISING

See, my servant shall prosper; he shall be exalted and lifted up, and shall be very high...

Who has believed what we have heard? And to whom has the arm of the Lord been revealed? For he grew up before him like a young plant, and like a root out of dry ground; he had no form or majesty that we should look at him, nothing in his appearance that we should desire him. He was despised and rejected by others; a man of suffering and acquainted with infirmity; and as one from whom others hide their faces he was despised, and we held him of no account. Surely he has borne our infirmities and carried our diseases; yet we accounted him stricken, struck down by God, and afflicted. But he was wounded for our transgressions, crushed for our iniquities; upon him was the punishment that made us whole, and by his bruises we are healed.

ISAIAH 52:13; 53:1–5

The parable of the lord and the servant is one of the most striking examples of Julian's reflections on her revelations. It is not mentioned at all in the early short text; it was given to her (perhaps not long after the original revelations) in response to her wrestling with the question of human sin and divine mercy. She did not immediately understand it fully, and in fact it was nearly 20 years later that she was told by God to consider every detail of the parable. In doing this, she came to a deeper understanding.

The parable that Julian originally saw begins with a lord, sitting down, and a servant standing beside him. The lord looks tenderly at the servant and sends him away to do his will. The servant loves the lord and sets off at speed, but in his hurry he falls into a deep ditch and injures himself badly. He is unable to help himself or even to turn his head and look at his lord. Julian considered carefully whether it was the servant's fault that he found himself in his predicament, and concluded that it was not: 'it was his own good will and great longing that had caused his fall'.[22]

As we will see in more detail tomorrow, the servant represents both Adam and Christ. As Adam, his fall stands for sin, which causes us to fall and makes us feel separated from God and often from our fellow human beings too. As Christ, his fall stands for the incarnation, for his coming down to earth to share in our human state. 'Adam fell from life to death, first into the depths of this wretched world, and then into hell. God's Son fell, with Adam, but into the depth of the Virgin's womb... with the intent of excusing Adam from blame both in heaven and on earth.'[23]

This excusing from blame was one of the key lessons for Julian from this parable. As she saw that the servant was not to blame for his fall, so she saw that the lord did not blame him either. He continued to look kindly on the servant, in two ways. The first was with natural compassion and pity, the second with delight in the thought of the reward that he was planning to give the servant: 'Here is my servant whom I love. What hurt and discomfort he has known in my service... Surely it would be right to reward him for all this terror and fright, this hurt, injury and grief?'[24]

This understanding is in line with Isaiah's prophecy as it continues beyond today's passage, especially in 53:11–12. Our falling is not wasted if it draws us closer to God and gives us a clearer sight of ourselves and of God: 'If we never fell we should never know how weak and wretched we are in ourselves; nor should we fully appreciate the astonishing love of our Maker.'[25]

This does not mean, however, that we should look lightly on sin or even believe that because it has, in God's grace, a positive outcome, we need not seek to avoid it. Julian warns against this, as did the Wesleys. It is a mistake to think that we should continue in sin so that grace may abound. No, says Julian, 'we should hate sin for Love's sake alone'.[26]

Julian is well known for seeing and addressing Jesus as our Mother, and in relation to sin she has a beautiful image. Our patient Mother wants us to do what any child does when in trouble—run to him, not run away in our shame. The church, too, is often called 'mother' and Julian uses this image to comfort us: 'the dear gracious hands of our Mother are ever about us, and eager to help'.[27]

PRAYER

Gracious Lord, look with pity and compassion on your servant. I often fall in your service, but even when I cannot see you, assure me of your presence and help me always to turn back to you, my brother, saviour, mother. Amen.

Wednesday

THE IMAGE OF CHRIST

So it is with the resurrection of the dead. What is sown is perishable, what is raised is imperishable. It is sown in dishonour, it is raised in glory. It is sown in weakness, it is raised in power. It is sown a physical body, it is raised a spiritual body. If there is a physical body, there is also a spiritual body. Thus it is written, 'The first man, Adam, became a living being'; the last Adam became a life-giving spirit. But it is not the spiritual that is first, but the physical, and then the spiritual. The first man was from the earth, a man of dust; the second man is from heaven. As was the man of dust, so are those who are of the dust; and as is the man of heaven, so are those who are of heaven. Just as we have borne the image of the man of dust, we will also bear the image of the man of heaven.

1 CORINTHIANS 15:42–49

Although she refers to herself as ignorant, Julian had obviously had some education, and was well grounded in the Bible. It is possible that she had spent some time with the Benedictine nuns at Carrow Abbey, near Norwich, and some think that she may have been a member of that community for a time. Certainly, her writing is steeped in biblical images and language, and she is concerned to be faithful to the teaching of the church, even as she wrestles with seeming incompatibilities between her revelations and what the church of her day taught.

In the parable of the lord and the servant, she draws in a very creative way on much of Paul's theology from today's passage in 1 Corinthians. So today I want to focus particularly on the identification of Christ with Adam, of Adam with all humankind, and therefore of Christ with all humankind.

'The incarnate Lord who suffers on the cross,' writes Michael McLean, 'is the new Adam, not just in the sense that in him is a new creation, but that in him God shares in the first Adam's fall.'[14] There is a sense here that we stand before a mirror, seeing first ourselves, then Adam, then Christ, shifting and dissolving into each other, at the same time maintaining their own identities and being wholly identified with each other.

Julian herself did not find the parable of the lord and servant easy to understand. Having received it, as she believed, as an answer to an anguished question about human sin and God's mercy, and how they could be made part of the one picture, she wrote at the end of the account of the original revelation, 'My puzzlement over the illustration never left me... The *servant* stood for Adam... but on the other hand there were many characteristics that could not possibly be ascribed to him. So there I had to leave it, a large part unknown.'[15]

In her later reflections, however, Julian began to see more clearly:

The servant that stood before the lord, I understood that he was showed for Adam, that is to say one man alone was shown at that time, and his falling, to make us understand thereby how God beholds anyone and his or her falling. For in the sight of God all men and women are as one person: that one person is all women, all men.[16]

Also, 'in the servant is comprehended the Second Person of the Trinity... The lord is the Father, God. The servant is the Son, Christ Jesus.'[17] Julian's stress on the humanity of Christ, as a guarantee that our own humanity is taken up into divinity, is characteristic of the 14th century in which she lived. Born probably in 1342, she inherited the fruits of a process that had been going on for several centuries, which resulted in what one author describes as 'an affective sensitized piety. There was a profound quest of the inner way, combined with a fundamental optimism about the universe'.[18]

We fall in Adam, but we are also raised in Adam, the second Adam, the beloved Son. Julian asserts boldly, 'Jesus is everyone that will be saved, and everyone that will be saved is Jesus',[19] but the ambivalence of the identification remains, with the shifting reflections in the mirror. Julian is always realistic as well as optimistic, and she acknowledges that 'in this life there is within us who are to be saved a surprising mixture of good and bad. We have our risen Lord; we have the wretchedness and mischief done by Adam's fall and death'.[20] This fluctuation, she says, will go on throughout our lives, but 'it is the will of God that we should trust that he is always with us'.[21]

PRAYER

Father, thank you for sending your Son, the second Adam, from heaven to share in our world of dust. In all my fluctuations, draw me to yourself, that I may come to bear in my earthly life the image of your life-giving Son, Jesus Christ our Lord. Amen.

Maundy Thursday

THE SERVANT KING

Now before the festival of the Passover, Jesus knew that his hour had come to depart from this world and go to the Father. Having loved his own who were in the world, he loved them to the end. The devil had already put it into the heart of Judas son of Simon Iscariot to betray him. And during supper Jesus, knowing that the Father had given all things into his hands, and that he had come from God and was going to God, got up from the table, took off his outer robe, and tied a towel around himself. Then he poured water into a basin and began to wash the disciples' feet and to wipe them with the towel that was tied around him...

After he had washed their feet, had put on his robe, and had returned to the table, he said to them, 'Do you know what I have done to you? You call me Teacher and Lord—and you are right, for that is what I am. So if I, your Lord and Teacher, have washed your feet, you also ought to wash one another's feet. For I have set you an example, that you also should do as I have done to you. Very truly, I tell you, servants are not greater than their master, nor are messengers greater than the one who sent them. If you know these things, you are blessed if you do them.'

JOHN 13:1–5, 12–17

Julian's choice of a solitary life may seem a selfish one. For around 45 years she lived alone in a small cell attached to the church of St Julian in Norwich, giving herself to prayer and to prolonged reflection on her revelations. In fact, though, she was not entirely isolated. She would have had a servant or two to do the practical tasks that she could not do herself, and there were two windows in her cell. One looked into the church, so that she could take part in the services held there. The other looked out on to the world, and people could come to this window to talk to Julian and seek her advice.

It is from someone who came to do just this that we have one of the few records of Julian outside her own book. In 1413, perhaps 38 years after Julian had entered her cell, a woman named Margery Kempe came to visit her, and wrote about the visit in her own book. Margery has been described as 'a psychologically tumultuous woman':[28] a native of King's Lynn in Norfolk, she experienced dramatic visions, spoke with Christ in her meditations, and went on many pilgrimages.

Julian was drawn by God to embrace solitude, not repulsed by the world. She still sought to serve the world in a manner compatible with her chosen way of life. This was a frequent concern for those advising people who took up the solitary life. 'Whose feet will you wash?' they asked, drawing on today's story of Jesus washing his disciples' feet. It contains one of the few direct commands to a particular action in the Gospels: 'You also should do as I have done to you.' In many churches, this command will be obeyed today as the priest washes the feet of the members of the congregation. I always find this a very moving ceremony, seeing the priest, the leader of the church family, kneeling at their feet and carrying out such a humble task.

This takes us back to Julian's parable of the lord and the servant. One of the striking things about the story can easily be missed if we are not aware of the times in which it was written. The lord does not treat the servant as a chattel, as property, as would have been normal in the feudal system. Instead, in his courtesy, he treats him as a valuable human being, watching over him when he falls and desiring to reward him for his sufferings in the lord's service.

In washing his disciples' feet, Jesus shows both courtesy and humility: he goes far beyond what any 'Lord and Teacher' would normally do for his students. But it was his choice to come as a servant, and Julian sees this symbolized in the servant's clothing in the parable: a skimpy, threadbare, plain white smock. She sees that 'the white smock is his flesh; its plainness, that there is nothing between the Godhead and the manhood; its straitness, his poverty; its age comes from Adam's wearing'.[29]

Jesus, in the incarnation, took on this humble clothing; in washing his disciples' feet, he put aside even this, 'taking the form of a slave' (Philippians 2:7). No wonder the lord, the Father, 'looks upon his servant [Christ] with very sweet and loving gaze'.[30]

PRAYER

Servant God, show me today whose feet I am called to wash, and give me grace to serve with courtesy and humility. Amen.

Good Friday

COMPASSION AND CONTRITION

It was nine o'clock in the morning when they crucified him. The inscription of the charge against him read, 'The King of the Jews'. And with him they crucified two bandits, one on his right and one on his left. Those who passed by derided him, shaking their heads and saying, 'Aha! You who would destroy the temple and build it in three days, save yourself, and come down from the cross!' In the same way the chief priests, along with the scribes, were also mocking him among themselves and saying, 'He saved others; he cannot save himself. Let the Messiah, the King of Israel, come down from the cross now, so that we may see and believe.' Those who were crucified with him also taunted him.

When it was noon, darkness came over the whole land until three in the afternoon. At three o'clock Jesus cried out with a loud voice, 'Eloi, Eloi, lema sabachthani?' which means, 'My God, my God, why have you forsaken me?' When some of the bystanders heard it, they said, 'Listen, he is calling for Elijah.' And someone ran, filled a sponge with sour wine, put it on a stick, and gave it to him to drink, saying, 'Wait, let us see whether Elijah will come to take him down.' Then Jesus gave a loud cry and breathed his last.

MARK 15:25–37

It was on 8 May 1373 that Julian experienced the revelations which shaped the rest of her life. This would have been in the Easter season, and the events of Good Friday would still have been fresh in her mind.

Some time before this, she had asked for three gifts. The original text of her book begins, 'I desired three gifts by the grace of God. The first was for an experience of Christ's passion; the second was for a bodily sickness; and the third was to receive, as a gift from God, three wounds.'[31] Later in the chapter, she specifies the wounds: 'the wound of contrition, the wound of compassion, and the wound of earnest longing'.[32]

This prayer was wonderfully answered in her experience of May 1373. She became sick, and was thought to be dying. Her priest brought a crucifix and placed it before her, so that she could meditate on the death of her Saviour as she herself died. In fact, as she did this, all pain left her, and she remembered the second wound she had asked for, that of compassion—literally 'suffering with'. 'I desired his pain to become my pain through compassion, followed by a greater closeness with God.'[33]

Then began the series of visions. Many were of details of the passion, details that are not given in the Gospel accounts, but which kindled her compassion and strengthened her love. First she saw the crown of thorns, with blood 'hot, fresh, plentiful, and lifelike'[34] trickling down from it. Then she saw the discolouration of Christ's face, and then the bleeding of his body from the scourging before the crucifixion. Then she saw Christ drawing close to death, his face 'dry and bloodless with a deadly pallor; then, through suffering, still more deathly pale'.[35] The drying of his body and the thirst that accompanied it are described vividly: 'The blessed body dried over a long period of time—with wrenching of the nails; with the weight of the head and body; with the cold wind's blowing.'[36]

These vivid visions were only one of the ways in which Julian experienced God during her revelations. She describes three ways in which God taught her: 'by bodily sight, by words formed in my understanding, and by ghostly [that is, spiritual] sight'.[37] Her writings are always clear about which of the three ways was operating at any time, and she makes it clear that she has recorded her experiences as precisely as she can: 'I have described the bodily sights as accurately as I can, and I have repeated the words exactly as our lord presented them to me. I have recounted the ghostly sights partially, but can never fully describe them.'[38]

Although her vision of the details of the passion was a painful experience, yet it also brought joy to Julian as she realized more fully Christ's great love for her and for all people. Her 'seeings' were interspersed with words and spiritual sights, which helped her in this. After she had seen the blood of the scourging, she relates, 'Then, without voice and without opening of lips, these words were formed in my soul: "Herewith is the fiend overcome."'[39] She saw God scorning the fiend's malice, and 'laughed mightily',[40] and she ends the chapter with words that sum up powerfully the mixed emotions of Good Friday: 'I see three things: joy, scorn and passion. I see joy that the fiend is overcome; I see scorn because God scorns him, and he shall be scorned; and I see passion, that he is overcome by the suffering and death so passionately sought and endured by our lord Jesus Christ.'[41]

PRAYER

Loving Jesus, as I contemplate your passion today, give me contrition, compassion and earnest longing for you. Amen.

Saturday

WAITING WITH CHRIST'S LOVERS

There were also women looking on from a distance; among them were Mary Magdalene, and Mary the mother of James the younger and of Joses, and Salome. These used to follow him and provided for him when he was in Galilee; and there were many other women who had come up with him to Jerusalem.

When evening had come, and since it was the day of Preparation, that is, the day before the sabbath, Joseph of Arimathea, a respected member of the council, who was also himself waiting expectantly for the kingdom of God, went boldly to Pilate and asked for the body of Jesus. Then Pilate wondered if he were already dead; and summoning the centurion, he asked him whether he had been dead for some time. When he learned from the centurion that he was dead, he granted the body to Joseph. Then Joseph bought a linen cloth, and taking down the body, wrapped it in the linen cloth, and laid it in a tomb that had been hewn out of the rock. He then rolled a stone against the door of the tomb. Mary Magdalene and Mary the mother of Joses saw where the body was laid.

MARK 15:40–47

Julian linked the first gift she asked from God—experience of Christ's passion—to the women who watched Jesus suffer and die. She explains:

As for the first, although I believed I already had some feeling for Christ's passion, yet I desired more by the grace of God. I thought at that time to be

like Mary Magdalen and others who were Christ's lovers, and therefore I
desired a bodily sight wherein I might have more knowledge of the bodily
pains of our Saviour, and of the compassion of our Lady and all his true
lovers that saw his pains in that time; for I would be one with them and
suffer with him.[42]

She is honest enough to admit that when this prayer was being
fulfilled, she had moments of regret. When she describes the drying
of Christ's body, which, in the longer text, she does with what one
modern translator describes as 'vivid, almost intrusive realism',[43]
she writes:

To see all these many pains of Christ filled me full of pain… Until I
thought to myself: 'Little did I realize what pain it was I asked for', and
like a wretch I regretted it, thinking to myself if only I had known what it
were like, I would never have prayed for it.[44]

She does not draw back, however, and is rewarded with a new level
of understanding of the cost of loving. She sees Mary the mother of
Christ as the supreme example of this.

For Christ and she were so united in love that the greatness of his loving
was to cause her very great pain… For however much higher, mightier,
sweeter the love is, the more sorrow it is to the lover to see the body they
love in pain. All his disciples, all his true lovers suffered pains more than
their own body's death.[45]

Many of us will be able to remember examples from our own
experience. The pain of watching someone whom we love suffer,
and being helpless to alleviate that suffering, is particularly sharp.
Parents seeing their child suffer, or husbands and wives seeing the
other in pain, will often say, 'I wish I could suffer for them.' So it is,
Julian says, with Christ and humankind: 'And in this I saw a great
oneing between Christ and ourselves; I knew it to be so: for when
he was in pain, we were in pain.'[46]

This compassion, this suffering with the other, is of course reciprocated by Christ. At the end of her vivid visions of the crucifixion, Julian thought that Christ had died. But then she saw his face change ('his countenance became joyous'[47]), and heard him ask, 'Are you pleased I suffered for you?' She replied, 'Yes, dear Lord, in your mercy: yes, good Lord, bless you always.' The conversation continued with Jesus replying, 'If you are pleased, then I too am pleased. This is my joy, my bliss, my endless liking that I was ever able to suffer for you. For truly, if I could have suffered more, I would have suffered more.'[48]

Although the pain that Julian saw and experienced as she stood by the cross of Christ with 'all his true lovers' was real, the love that brought Jesus to that cross was more real. The love and the suffering are not separate, but love overcomes suffering because it is more deeply rooted in the nature of what God has created. 'For the pain was a deed done in time by the working of love, but his love was without beginning, and is and ever shall be without any end.'[49]

PRAYER

Crucified Saviour, as I remember what you suffered for me, fill my heart with compassion for the sufferings of the world that you died to redeem. Keep me always in the assurance that love is stronger than pain and death, even when all my hope lies in the tomb. Amen.

Easter Sunday

LOVE STRONGER THAN DEATH

Early on the first day of the week, while it was still dark, Mary Magdalene came to the tomb and saw that the stone had been removed from the tomb. So she ran and went to Simon Peter and the other disciple, the one whom Jesus loved, and said to them, 'They have taken the Lord out of the tomb, and we do not know where they have laid him.' Then Peter and the other disciple set out and went towards the tomb. The two were running together, but the other disciple outran Peter and reached the tomb first. He bent down to look in and saw the linen wrappings lying there, but he did not go in. Then Simon Peter came, following him, and went into the tomb. He saw the linen wrappings lying there, and the cloth that had been on Jesus' head, not lying with the linen wrappings but rolled up in a place by itself. Then the other disciple, who reached the tomb first, also went in, and he saw and believed.

JOHN 20:1–8

Every year, Easter Day surprises me somehow. The joy of the resurrection makes itself known in some new and unexpected way; the birds beginning to sing as we light the new fire outdoors and prepare to make our way into the darkened chapel bearing the light of Christ; the singing of the Exultet as we stand round the Paschal candle, with its famous line 'O happy fault, O necessary sin of Adam'; the noisy Gloria as we bang drums and ring bells, and add alleluias to everything after the long weeks of Lent without them.

Somehow, the triumph of life over death is always fresh, however many Lents I have been through, and however much I think that I've done it all before. Words fail me, and my heart dances.

At the end of Julian's parable of the lord and the servant, she gives a vivid picture of this transformation.

His body was in the grave until the Easter morrow, and from that time he never lay no more; for then truly was an end to the wallowing and writhing, the groaning and moaning; and our foul mortal flesh that God's Son took upon himself, which was Adam's old smock, straight, threadbare, and short, then by our Saviour was made fair: now white, bright and of endless cleanness, wide and full, more fair, more rich than the clothing which I saw on the Father. For that clothing was blue and Christ's clothing is now fine and dazzling, a many-colour mix so marvellous it may not be described, it is so worshipful.[50]

So the servant is rewarded as the lord had intended for his service and his suffering. In fact, his fall (O happy fault!) earns him a better reward than he would have had if he had not fallen in the first place.

The natural consequence of [God's] great goodness and worth was that his much beloved servant should be truly and gladly rewarded beyond anything he could have had had he not fallen. Yes, indeed, further; his fall and subsequent suffering were to be transformed into great and superlative honour and everlasting joy.[51]

Because we are bound up in Christ, the second Adam, as well as in the first Adam, we too are to be rewarded for our service and our suffering. Our longing for God is only a pale shadow of God's longing for us. Julian sees Christ's thirst on the cross as both physical and spiritual, and says of the spiritual, 'His thirst and loving longing is to have us all, integrated in him, to his great enjoyment… And in virtue of this longing which is in Christ we in turn long for him too. No soul comes to heaven without it.'[52]

Our sharing in the passion of Christ is not intended to increase our guilt and shame, but to convince us ever more of the great love that God has for us, and to awaken in us an answering love. Julian speaks of choosing 'Jesus for my heaven. I wanted no other heaven than Jesus, who will be my joy when I do eventually get there.'[53]

Here and now, life often puzzles us, and it can be hard to sustain our faith in God. In our times of doubt we often add to our pain by berating ourselves for our lack of faith, and imagine that God is judging us and disapproving of us, but Julian sees it differently: 'Notwithstanding our foolishness and blindness here below, our courteous Lord always has regard for us, rejoicing at this work in our souls.'[54]

This work is the work of love, which is stronger than death (Song of Solomon 8:6), and Julian's revelations and her many years of reflection are summed up in her final chapter.

So it was that I learned that love was our Lord's meaning. And I saw for certain, both here and elsewhere, that before ever he made us, God loved us; and that his love has never slackened, nor ever shall. In this love all his works have been done, and in this love he has made everything serve us; and in this love our life is everlasting. Our beginning was when we were made, but the love in which he made us never had beginning. In it we have our beginning.[55]

Love's redeeming work is done, alleluia!

PRAYER

Lord of life, bring me to my glorious resurrection, and hold me in your love for ever. Amen.

THE JOURNEY CONTINUES

Now on that same day two of them were going to a village called Emmaus, about seven miles from Jerusalem, and talking with each other about all these things that had happened. While they were talking and discussing, Jesus himself came near and went with them, but their eyes were kept from recognizing him. And he said to them, 'What are you discussing with each other while you walk along?' They stood still, looking sad. Then one of them, whose name was Cleopas, answered him, 'Are you the only stranger in Jerusalem who does not know the things that have taken place there in these days?' He asked them, 'What things?' They replied, 'The things about Jesus of Nazareth, who was a prophet mighty in deed and word before God and all the people…' Then he said to them, 'Oh, how foolish you are, and how slow of heart to believe all that the prophets have declared…' Then beginning with Moses and all the prophets, he interpreted to them the things about himself in all the scriptures.

As they came near the village to which they were going, he walked ahead as if he were going on. But they urged him strongly, saying, 'Stay with us, because it is almost evening and the day is now nearly over.' So he went in to stay with them. When he was at the table with them, he took bread, blessed and broke it, and give it to them. Then their eyes were opened, and they recognized him; and he vanished from their sight. They said to each other, 'Were not our hearts burning within us while he was talking to us on the road, while he was opening the scriptures to us?'

LUKE 24:13–19, 25, 27–32

When we reach Easter Monday, it's easy to breathe a sigh of relief that it's all over for another year, that we can gratefully give up whatever extra discipline or self-denial we may have taken on for Lent, that the intensity of Holy Week and its special services can give way to 'normality'.

But this story doesn't allow us to do that. It suggests strongly that the journey of Lent doesn't end in the garden, with the empty tomb, with the variously doubting and believing disciples. The empty tomb is another station on the pilgrimage of the Christian life— a very important one but, like all the stations, a place to pass through, not to settle down in. The angels in Mark's account of the resurrection tell the grieving women, 'He has been raised; he is not here… he is going ahead of you' (Mark 16:6b–7).

In the Emmaus resurrection story, we have a powerful and moving picture of Jesus coming alongside two of his disciples on the road (and notice that they are not of the inner circle of the apostles). He walks with them, he is concerned about their sadness, and he continues to be their teacher as he was in life.

He responds to their desire for his continued company—'Stay with us'—and joins them for a meal. In the familiar gesture of taking, blessing and breaking bread, at last their eyes are opened, and they recognize their companion on the road. Then they can recognize also that he had kindled their hearts in his teaching on the scriptures, in the way he helped them to see afresh the familiar stories of patriarchs and prophets and the history of their people.

I find this a marvellous parable for the Christian life. While most of us will have times set aside for prayer, for coming together in worship and fellowship, perhaps for solitude or for study, most of it happens 'on the road'. As we travel, we can be preoccupied with our own interpretation of what is happening to us and around us, trying to make the best sense of it that we can, but remaining blind to the ways in which Jesus comes alongside us and travels with us. As he travels with us, he makes himself known in word and sacrament—in the opening of the scriptures, and the breaking of the bread.

Jesus is, of course, the most important companion on our journey, but he is not the only one. We are given our families and friends and fellow Christians—those who support and challenge and teach us—and not only those who are physically present with us, but also those who have taken the journey before us and have recorded something of what they discovered. The company of our fellow travellers extends through time and space, and we never travel alone, however it may feel.

Some figures from the past draw alongside us for a short time, with a particular lesson to teach or insight to share. Others become constant companions, to whom we turn again and again. It is my hope that some of those whom you have met during this Lenten journey together may remain with you on the road, for a longer or shorter time, opening the scriptures to you, opening your eyes to Jesus, and feeding you with the bread of life.

PRAYER

Risen Lord, continue to walk with me as I go on my journey, and send your friends and lovers to be my companions. Amen.

PRAYING THE PASSION

Spend a significant amount of time, on at least one day this week, praying the passion. Read one of the Gospel accounts slowly, pausing to engage your senses, your imagination, your mind and your heart in the story as it unfolds. Different people will find different ways of doing this more fruitful.

For some, visualizing the scenes will bring them most vividly alive. You might like to use art too, finding portrayals of certain scenes from artists who speak to you and using them as a way into the story. You may find it fruitful to make your own visual response to the story; you don't have to be an artist to use colours and shapes to express your response.

For some, it will be the words that speak to them. Whenever particular phrases or sentences catch your attention, pause and repeat them, ruminating on them, not rushing on to the next passage. Some words may lead you into a dialogue with God in prayer. Others may lead you to reflect in writing in your own journal, or to a piece of creative writing that shares something of your experience with others.

For others, music may be the way in. Sing your favourite passion hymns, listen to one of the famous settings of the passion, such as Bach's *St Matthew* or *St John Passion*, or one of those by Heinrich Schütz, and let your heart be moved by what you hear.

For others again, it may be most powerful simply to spend time standing by the cross, silently, keeping company with Christ in his suffering.

SOLITUDE AND SERVICE

Julian lived a particular combination of these two dimensions of life, much nearer the 'solitude' end of the continuum than most people experience. As we have seen, however, even in her commitment to an extreme form of solitude, she had a concern for others and found ways of serving them.

If we see solitude as representing the inner life, and service as representing engagement with the world, where are you on the continuum at the moment? It's easy to think that the middle must be the right place to be, but this is not necessarily the case. Each person is unique and has a unique calling from God, and this will involve differing amounts of these aspects of life. But each life needs some measure of each.

Is your place on the continuum the right one for you now? As your circumstances change, it may be right and necessary to shift towards one end or the other. Do you need to do some rebalancing?

GOD SPEAKING

How do you experience God communicating with you? Do Julian's three ways—bodily sight, words formed in the understanding, spiritual sight—echo anything of your experience? They are not the only ways in which God can speak. Some people find God communicating much more through the created world, through other people, or through the events of their life.

Look back on your experiences of God speaking to you this Lent. Perhaps you have kept a journal and can read your entries and pick out what is particularly significant. Follow Julian's example and keep on reflecting on these 'revelations'. Give thanks for what has nourished you in them, and pray for clarification of what you still find puzzling. Like Julian, you may have to wait for the answers, so be prepared to persevere, and keep listening.

CONTINUING THE JOURNEY

If you want to continue the journey you have begun this Lent with any of the companions in this book, here are some suggestions for further reading, and some places to visit. The books listed in the References (pp. 187–90) may also be of interest.

THOMAS TRAHERNE

Thomas Traherne, *Poetry and Prose* (Denise Inge, ed.), SPCK, 2002. Includes both familiar and newly discovered work, along with an introduction to Traherne's life and work.

Thomas Traherne, *Centuries of Meditations*, The Shrine of Wisdom, 2002.

BEDE

Benedicta Ward SLG, *The Venerable Bede*, Geoffrey Chapman, 1990. A comprehensive account of Bede's writings, located against his life and times. Contains a good bibliography of his writings, many of which have not yet been translated from the original Latin.

Two books that have been translated are:

Bede, *A History of the English Church and People* (Leo Sherley-Price, trans.), Penguin, 1990.

J.F. Webb (trans.), *The Age of Bede*, Penguin, 1965. Contains Bede's *Life of Cuthbert*, and *Lives of the Abbots of Wearmouth and Jarrow*.

Benedicta Ward SLG, *Bede and the Psalter*, SLG Press, 2002. Pamphlet, originally given as a lecture in Jarrow.

Benedicta Ward SLG, *High King of Heaven: Aspects of Early English Spirituality*, Mowbray, 1999. Not just on Bede, but useful for a wider view of his times.

Benedicta Ward SLG (ed.), *Christ Within Me: Daily Readings from the Anglo-Saxon Tradition*, DLT, 1999. Sadly appears to be out of print at the time of writing.

Visit Jarrow. Bede's World (www.bedesworld.co.uk) includes St Paul's Church, whose chancel was part of Bede's monastery, an exhibition on the Age of Bede, an Anglo-Saxon demonstration farm, and herb garden.

AELRED OF RIEVAULX

Aelred of Rievaulx, *The Way of Friendship: Selected Spiritual Writings* (M. Basil Pennington, ed.), New City Press, 2001. Excerpts from a number of Aelred's books, arranged under subject headings. Contains a good bibliography of his works and books about him.

Aelred of Rievaulx, *Spiritual Friendship* (Mary Eugenia Laker, trans.), SSND, Cistercian Publications, 1977 (who also publish a number of other works).

Aelred Squire OP, *Aelred of Rievaulx: A Study*, Cistercian Publications, 1994

Pauline Matarasso (trans., ed.), *The Cistercian World: Monastic Writings of the Twelfth Century*, Penguin, 1993. For the wider view of Aelred's times and other Cistercians.

Visit Rievaulx, near Helmsley in North Yorkshire. Some of the abbey ruins date from Aelred's time, and the setting is very beautiful. Details from www.english-heritage.org.uk

THE CLOUD OF UNKNOWING

Clifton Wolters (trans.), *The Cloud of Unknowing and Other Works*, Penguin, 1978. The other works are *The Epistle of Privy Counsel*, *Dionysius' Mystical Teaching*, and *The Epistle of Prayer*.

William Johnston (ed.), *The Cloud of Unknowing and the Book of Privy Counselling*, Bantam Doubleday, 1996.

Robert Way (comp.), *The Wisdom of the English Mystics*, Sheldon Press, 1978. Contains stories and sayings from a wide range of English mystics, including the *Cloud* author, Julian, Aelred and Traherne (o/p).

Thomas Keating, *Foundations for Centering Prayer and the Christian Contemplative Life*, Continuum, 2002. (Combines *Open Mind: Open Heart*, *Invitation to Love* and *The Mystery of the Liturgy* in a single volume.) Thomas Keating is one of the founders of Centering Prayer and this volume contains the heart of his teaching.

Cynthia Bourgeault, *Centering Prayer and Inner Awakening*, Cowley Publications, 2004. For me, this is the clearest teaching on Centering Prayer; especially valuable if you already have experience of other forms of contemplative prayer, as she explains very clearly the differences between Centering Prayer and other forms.

M. Basil Pennington, *Centering Prayer: Renewing an Ancient Christian Prayer Form*, Image Books, 1982. Another of the founders, with his own perspective on the practice.

www.centeringprayer.com is the website of Contemplative Outreach, an organization founded by Thomas Keating. All of his books are available here, along with articles, newsletters and a wealth of other information.

www.contemplative.org is the website of Cynthia Bourgeault, who runs an ecumenical organization aiming to encourage a deepening of contemplative prayer.

JOHN AND CHARLES WESLEY

John and Charles Wesley, *Selected Writings and Hymns*, Paulist Press, 1981. A good selection from the work of both brothers, with a substantial introduction.

Charles Wesley, *A Reader* (John R. Tyson, ed.), OUP, 2000. A chronologically arranged selection of his many writings, which outline his life and illuminate his thought.

Paul Wesley Chilcote, *Recapturing the Wesleys' Vision: An Introduction to the Faith of John and Charles Wesley*, Intervarsity Press, 2004.

Roy Hattersley, *John Wesley: A Brand from the Burning*, Time Warner Books Abacus, 2004. A prize-winning biography.

Gordon S. Wakefield, *Methodist Spirituality*, SCM Press, 1999. Reprinting at the time of preparation of this book.

Visit Epworth Rectory, where the Wesleys were born. It is open from March to October; details from www.epwortholdrectory.org.uk

Wesley's Chapel, City Road, London is still in use as a place of worship and can be visited, as can his house nearby and the Museum of Methodism. Information about all of them can be found at www.wesleyschapel.org.uk

JOHN DONNE

There are many editions of Donne's works available; two are given in the References. Although Donne is best known as a poet, it is well worth trying his prose as well.

David L. Edwards, *John Donne: Man of Flesh and Spirit*, Eerdmans, 2002 (hardback), 2005 (paperback). A highly regarded biography.

John Carey, *John Donne: Life, Mind and Art*, Faber and Faber, 1990. Covers Donne's life and work.

Visit St Paul's Cathedral in London, where the statue of Donne in his shroud can still be seen.

JULIAN OF NORWICH

There are many editions of the *Revelations* available; these are just a few:

Showings, Edmund Colledge OSA and James Walsh SJ (ed. and trans.), SPCK (Classics of Western Spirituality series), 1978. Contains both texts, and a long and valuable introduction.

Revelations of Divine Love, Clifton Wolters (trans.), Penguin, 1966. The Long Text in modern English.

Revelation of Love, John Skinner (trans.), Doubleday, 1996. The Long Text in modern English.

The Revelations of Divine Love, James Walsh SJ, Anthony Clarke (trans.), 1961. The Long Text, modernized but much nearer to the Middle English original than the others.

Revelations: Motherhood of God, Frances Beer (trans.), DS Brewer, 1998. The Short Text, plus five chapters from the Long Text which deal with the motherhood of God.

Books about Julian

Robert Llewelyn (ed.), *Julian, Woman of her Day*, DLT, 1985. A collection of essays by a variety of authors. Out of print, but well worth trying to borrow or finding a second-hand copy.

Robert Llewelyn, *With Pity, Not with Blame*, DLT, 1982. On Julian's way of contemplative prayer; also includes a chapter on *The Cloud of Unknowing*.

Grace Jantzen, *Julian of Norwich: Mystic and Theologian*, SPCK, 2000. Sets out to integrate scholarly findings with contemporary spirituality, and to set Julian's theology against the background of her world and her chosen life as an anchoress, living in permanent solitude in a small cell attached to a church.

Ritamary Bradley, *Not for the Wise: The Prayer Texts of Julian of Norwich*, DLT, 1994. Julian's passages of prayer with a commentary on each, intended to help the reader apply them in their own life.

Visit Norwich, where the rebuilt hermitage attached to the church of St Julian, not far from the centre of Norwich, is kept as a place of prayer and pilgrimage. The shrine administrator has a website: www.home.clara.net/frmartinsmith/julian

REFERENCES

Quotations in this book are taken from the following sources. The initials given before each title are the key to the endnotes on pages 191–92. Books marked 'o/p' are now out of print, but you may be able to borrow them through your local library, or find a copy through an online bookseller.

INTRODUCTION

GL   Joan M. Nuth, *God's Lovers in an Age of Anxiety: The Medieval English Mystics*, DLT, 2001

THOMAS TRAHERNE

AL   Adrian Leak, 'Metaphysical poet, enjoys socialising', *Church Times*, 8 October 2004, p. 15

BN   John Davies, *Beginning Now*, Collins, 1971 (o/p)

EH   The English Hymnal, OUP, 1933

LoG   A.M. Allchin (ed.), *Landscapes of Glory: Daily Readings with Thomas Traherne*, DLT, 1989

OBCV   David Cecil (ed.), *The Oxford Book of Christian Verse*, OUP, 1940 (o/p, but there is a *New Oxford Book of Christian Verse*, Donald Davie (ed.), in print.

OBMV   D.H.S. Nicholson and A.H.E. Lee, *The Oxford Book of English Mystical Verse*, OUP, 1917

SoH   Denise Inge, 'A Sight of Happiness: Thomas Traherne's Felicity in a Fleeting World', *The Way*, Vol. 44, no. 1, January 2005, pp. 75–87

WEM   Robert Way, *The Wisdom of the English Mystics*, Sheldon Press, 1978 (o/p)

VENERABLE BEDE

AOB   J.F. Webb (trans.), *The Age of Bede*, Penguin, 1965

BP   Benedicta Ward, *Bede and the Psalter*, SLG Press, 2002

CC   Henry Mayr-Harting, *The Coming of Christianity to Anglo-Saxon England*, Pennsylvania State University Press, 1991

CWM   Benedicta Ward (ed.), *Christ Within Me: Daily Readings from the Anglo-Saxon Tradition*, DLT, 1999 (o/p)

HECP   Bede, *A History of the English Church and People*, Penguin, 1990

HKH   Benedicta Ward, *High King of Heaven: Aspects of Early English Spirituality*, Mowbray, 1999

OFK   T.H. White, *The Once and Future King*, HarperCollins, 1996

VB   Benedicta Ward, *The Venerable Bede*, Geoffrey Chapman, 1990 (o/p)

AELRED OF RIEVAULX

AoR   Aelred Squire OP, *Aelred of Rievaulx: A Study*, SPCK, 1969

CW   Pauline Matarasso (trans., ed.), *The Cistercian World: Monastic Writings of the Twelfth Century*, Penguin, 1993

GL   Joan M. Nuth, *God's Lovers in an Age of Anxiety: the Medieval English Mystics*, DLT, 2001

MTA   Amédée Hallier, *The Monastic Theology of Aelred of Rievaulx*, Irish University Press, 1969 (Cistercian Studies Series no. 2) (o/p)

SF   Aelred, *Spiritual Friendship*, Cistercian Publications, 1977

TSG   Brendan Callaghan, 'Traditions of Spiritual Guidance: Aelred of Rievaulx', *The Way*, Vol. 38, no. 4, October 1998, pp. 375–387

WF   Aelred, *The Way of Friendship; Selected Spiritual Writings* (M. Basil, ed.), Pennington, New City Press, 2001

WS   Esther de Waal, *The Way of Simplicity: the Cistercian Tradition*, DLT, 1998

THE CLOUD OF UNKNOWING

CUJ   William Johnston (ed.), *The Cloud of Unknowing and the Book of Privy Counselling*, Image Books, 1973

CUP   Clifton Wolters (trans.), *The Cloud of Unknowing and Other Works*, Penguin, 1978

DMT   *Dionysius' Mystical Teaching* (in CUP)

DS   Robert W. Englert, 'Traditions of Spiritual Guidance: Desire and Symbol—Two Aspects of the Cloud of Unknowing', *The Way*, Vol. 41, no. 1, January 2001, pp. 52–60

EP   *The Epistle of Prayer* (in CUP)

GL   Joan M. Nuth, *God's Lovers in an Age of Anxiety: The Medieval English Mystics*, DLT, 2001

PC   *The Epistle of Privy Counsel* (in CUP)

PCU   Robert W. Englert, 'Traditions of Spiritual Guidance: Penance in the Cloud of Unknowing', *The Way*, Vol. 38, no. 2, April 1998, pp. 170–78

JOHN AND CHARLES WESLEY

EH   *The English Hymnal*, OUP, 1933

FoL   Gordon Wakefield, *Fire of Love: The Spirituality of John Wesley*, DLT, 1976 (o/p)

HP   *Hymns and Psalms*, Methodist Publishing House, 1983

JCW   John and Charles Wesley, *Selected Writings and Hymns*, Paulist Press, 1981

JWM   Gordon S. Wakefield, 'Traditions of Spiritual Guidance: John Wesley and the Methodist System', *The Way*, Vol. 31, no. 1, January 1991, pp. 69–79

SH   Leslie Griffiths, 'Traditions of Spiritual Guidance: Spirituality and the Hymns of Charles Wesley', *The Way*, Vol. 31, no. 4, October 1991, pp. 331–340

JOHN DONNE

DEO John Donne, *Devotions upon Emergent Occasions, together with Death's Duel*, University of Michigan Press, 1960

GF Giles Fraser, *Church Times*, 23 July 2004, p. 7

MoP *Masters of Prayer: John Donne* (foreword and notes by Mary Holtby), CIO Publishing, 1984 (o/p)

MW John Donne, *The Major Works*, OUP, 1990

PI L. William Countryman, *The Poetic Imagination: An Anglican Spiritual Tradition*, DLT, 1999

PJD Duane Arnold (comp.), *Praying with John Donne and George Herbert*, Triangle, 1991 (o/p)

SP John Donne, *Selected Poems* (John Hayward, ed.), Penguin, 1984

JULIAN OF NORWICH

JON Grace Jantzen, *Julian of Norwich*, SPCK, 1987 (o/p—see 'Continuing the Journey' for an updated edition)

JWD Robert Llewelyn (ed.), *Julian: Woman of our Day*, DLT, 1985 (o/p)

RDLB Julian of Norwich, *Revelations of Divine Love: The Motherhood of God, an Excerpt* (trans. and introd. Frances Beer), DS Brewer, 1998

RDLP Julian of Norwich, *Revelations of Divine Love* (Clifton Wolters, trans.), Penguin, 1966

RDLS Julian of Norwich, *Revelation of Love* (John Skinner, trans.), Doubleday, 1996

SMM Michael Mott, *The Seven Mountains of Thomas Merton*, Sheldon Press, 1986 (o/p)

NOTES

Introduction

1   GL p. 161

Thomas Traherne

1   SoH p. 77
2   AL
3   AL
4   LS pp. 225/6
5   SoH p. 79
6   WEM pp. 64/5
7   WEM p. 31
8   EH 94
9   OBMV p. 82
10 LoG p. 14
11 LoG pp. 14/15
12 LoG p. 28
13 OBCV p. 290
14 WEM p. 19
15 WEM p. 21
16 OBMV p. 63
17 OBCV p. 276
18 OBCV p. 285
19 SoH p. 78
20 SoH pp. 82/3
21 LoG p. 2
22 LoG p. 58
23 OBCV p. 271
24 LoG p. 58

Venerable Bede

1   HECP p. 329
2   HECP I:26
3   HECP I:27
4   HECP IV:23
5   CWM p. 5
6   AOB p. 218
7   HKH p. 40
8   CWM p. 27
9   CC p. 218
10 HECP p. 33

11 HECP p. 35
12 HECP I:32
13 CC p. 217
14 VB p. 43
15 VB p. 49
16 CWM p. 59
17 CWM p. 49
18 VB p. 78
19 CWM p. 3
20 CWM p. 39
21 HECP IV:2
22 CWM p. 4
23 HECP IV:18
24 CWM p. 47
25 BP p. 16
26 BP pp. 16/7
27 OFK p. 181

Aelred of Rievaulx

1   SF p. 12
2   SF 3:6, p 93
3   SF 2:20, 21, pp. 74/5
4   TSG p. 385
5   WF p. 107
6   WF p. 105
7   WF p. 105
8   WF p. 105
9   WF p. 108
10 WF pp. 73/4
11 WF p. 81
12 SF 3:133, p. 131
13 SF 1:1, p. 51
14 SF 1:8, p. 53
15 SF Prologue, p. 46
16 WF p. 87
17 WF p. 92
18 AoR p. 126
19 SF 2:21 p. 75
20 GL p. 16
21 SF p. 46
22 WS p. 59

23 TSG p. 379
24 CW p. 193
25 AoR p. 66
26 AoR p. 66
27 CW p. xv
28 WF p. 122
29 AoR p. 68
30 WF p. 110
31 WF p. 101
32 SF 1:57 p. 63
33 MTA p. 23
34 SF 3:82 p. 112
35 TSG p. 379
36 TSG p. 380
37 SF 3:127 p. 129
38 CW p. 165

The Cloud of Unknowing

1   PC Prologue p. 159
2   EP p. 232
3   CUP. 6, p. 68
4   GL p. 58
5   PC 4, p. 170
6   CUJ 75, p. 144/5
7   PC 11, pp. 193/4
8   CUJ 34 p. 91
9   CUJ 42 p. 101
10 CUJ 7, p. 56
11 CUJ 3 p. 48
12 CUJ 46 p. 106
13 CUJ 46 p. 107
14 CUP. 50 p. 120
15 CUJ 52 p. 115
16 CUJ 53 p. 116
17 CUP. 54 p. 12
18 CUJ 12 p. 64
19 CUP. 28 p. 96
20 CUJ 40 p. 99
21 DS pp. 164/5
22 CUJ 31 p. 88

23 CUP 32 p. 98
24 CUJ 32 p. 89
25 CUP 16 p. 81
26 CUP 2 p. 60
27 CUJ 1 p. 46
28 CUJ 9 pp. 60/1
29 CUP 12 p. 76
30 CUJ 29 p. 86
31 PC 8 p. 184
32 PC 8 p. 185
33 DS p. 58
34 PCU p. 175
35 DMT 1 p. 211
36 DMT 2 p. 212
37 DMT 3 p. 215
38 GL p. 57
39 CUJ 3 p. 49

John and Charles Wesley

1   JCW p. 106
2   JCW p. 107
3   JCW p. 5
4   JCW p. 107
5   JCW p. 329
6   EH 303
7   JCW p. 101
8   HP 434
9   JCW p. 37
10 JCW p. 38
11 FoL p. 60
12 FoL p. 64
13 JWM p. 72
14 JCW p. 34
15 FoL p. 42
16 FoL p. 43
17 FoL p. 57
18 HP 753
19 SH p. 339
20 SH p. 332/3
21 SH p. 332/3
22 SH p. 338
23 JWM p. 79
24 SH p. 336
25 JCW p. 299
26 JCW p. 144

27 JCW p. 387
28 JCW p. 386
29 HP 439
30 SH p. 339

John Donne

1   MW p. 65
2   SP 89
3   MW pp. 384/5
4   MW p. 271
5   MoP p. 8
6   PJD p. 11
7   MW p. 267
8   MW p. 268
9   MW p. 268
10 MW p. 276
11 DEO pp. 7/8
12 DEO p. 101
13 MW p. 174
14 GF
15 MW p. 280
16 MW p. 306
17 MW p. 104
18 DEO p. 109
19 DEO p. 109
20 MW p. 305
21 DEO p. 108
22 MW p. 265
23 MW p. 265
24 MW p. 383
25 PJD p. 38
26 MW p. 312
27 MW p. 302
28 PI p. 142

Julian of Norwich

1   SMM p. 362
2   JWD p xi
3   RDLB p. 33
4   RDLB p. 32
5   RDLP p. 105
6   RDLP p. 107
7   RDLS p. 92
8   RDLS p. 127
9   RDLB p. 66

10 REDL p. 68
11 RDLB p. 77
12 RDLB p. 61
13 RDLB p. 77
14 JWD p. 4
15 RDLP p. 143
16 RDLS p. 103
17 RDLS p. 108
18 JWD p 91
19 RDLP p. 149
20 RDLP p. 151
21 RDLP p. 152
22 RDLP p. 142
23 RDLP p. 148
24 RDLP p. 142
25 RDLP p. 172
26 RDLP p. 122
27 RDLP p. 173
28 JON p. 157
29 RDLS p. 109
30 RDLS p. 100
31 RDLB p. 25
32 RDLB p. 27
33 RDLB p. 28
34 RDLB p. 29
35 RDLB p. 38
36 RDLB p. 38
37 RDLB p. 33
38 RDLB p. 58
39 RDLB p. 35
40 RDLB p. 36
41 RDLB p. 36
42 RDLS p. 4
43 RDLS p. 36
44 RDLS p. 38
45 RDLS p. 39
46 RDLS p. 39
47 RDLB pp. 40/1
48 RDLS p. 46
49 RDLB p. 40
50 RDLS pp. 111/2
51 RDLP p. 143
52 RDLP pp. 108/9
53 RDLP pp 92/3
54 RDLP p. 210
55 RDLP p. 212